Picture Puzzles
Spot the Difference Book

This Book Belongs To:

_____

Hello!

Many thanks for your purchase and we hope that you enjoy this book.

You are most welcome to leave a review as it lets us know how we are doing and make any improvements where required.

For all enquires, please send an email to info@starshinebright.com.au

Puzzle 1

Find 3 differences in the picture below.

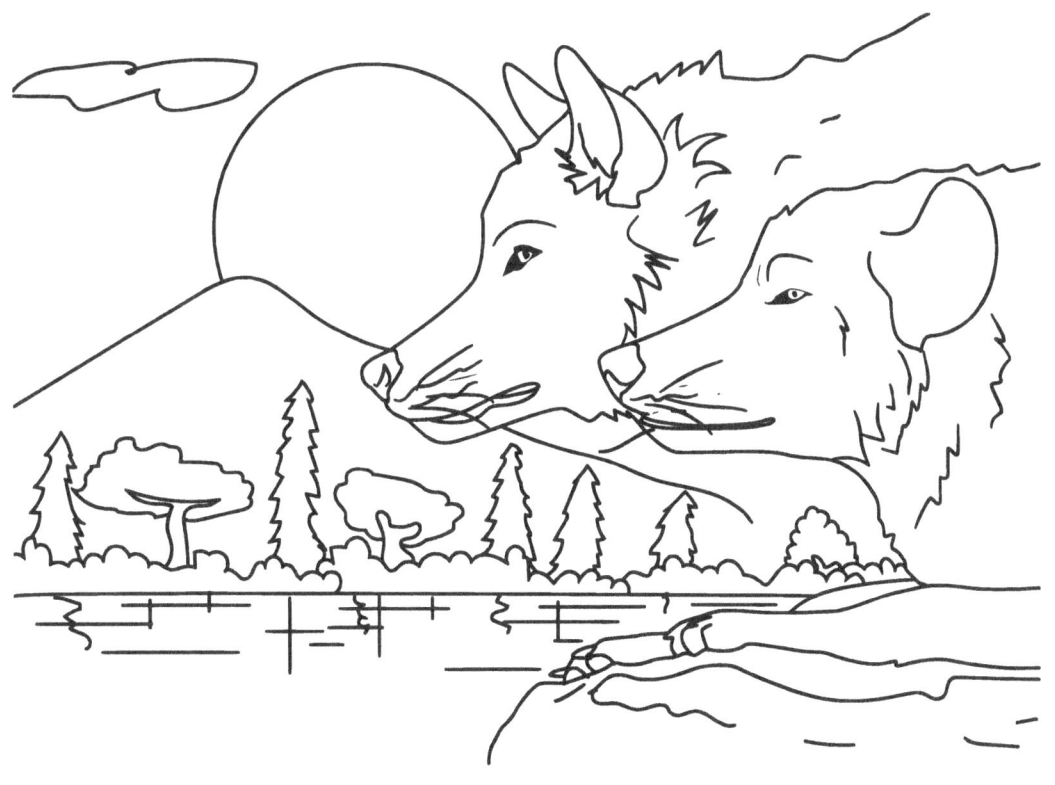

Puzzle 2

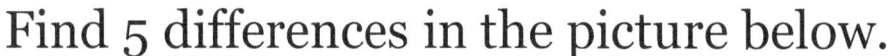

Find 5 differences in the picture below.

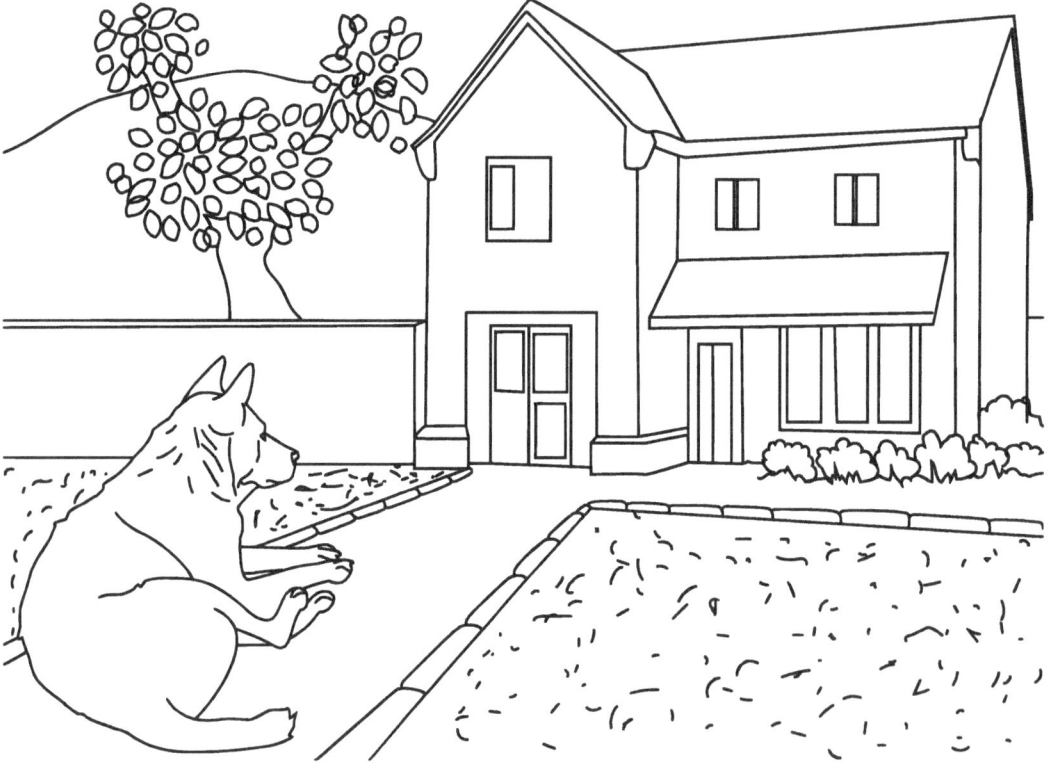

Puzzle 3

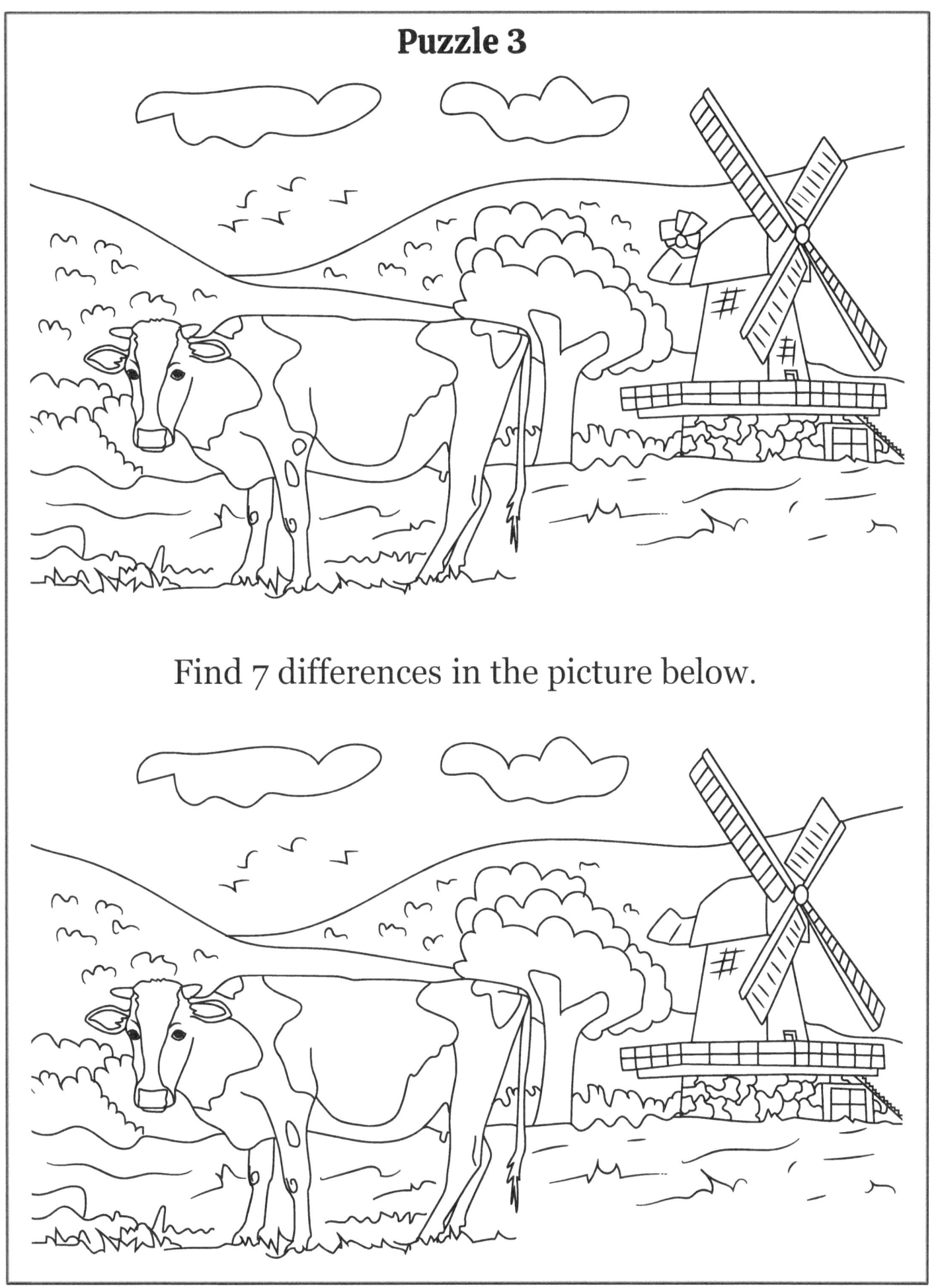

Find 7 differences in the picture below.

Puzzle 4

Find 4 differences in the picture below.

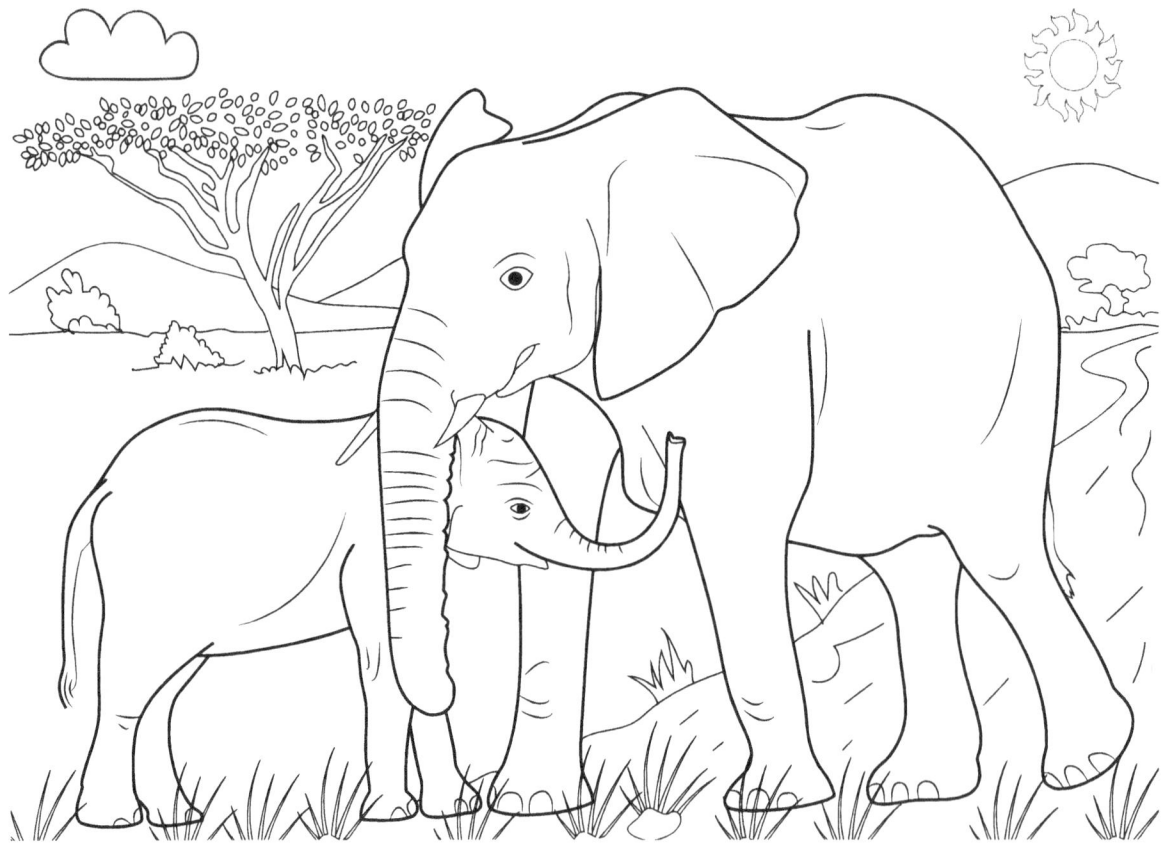

Puzzle 5

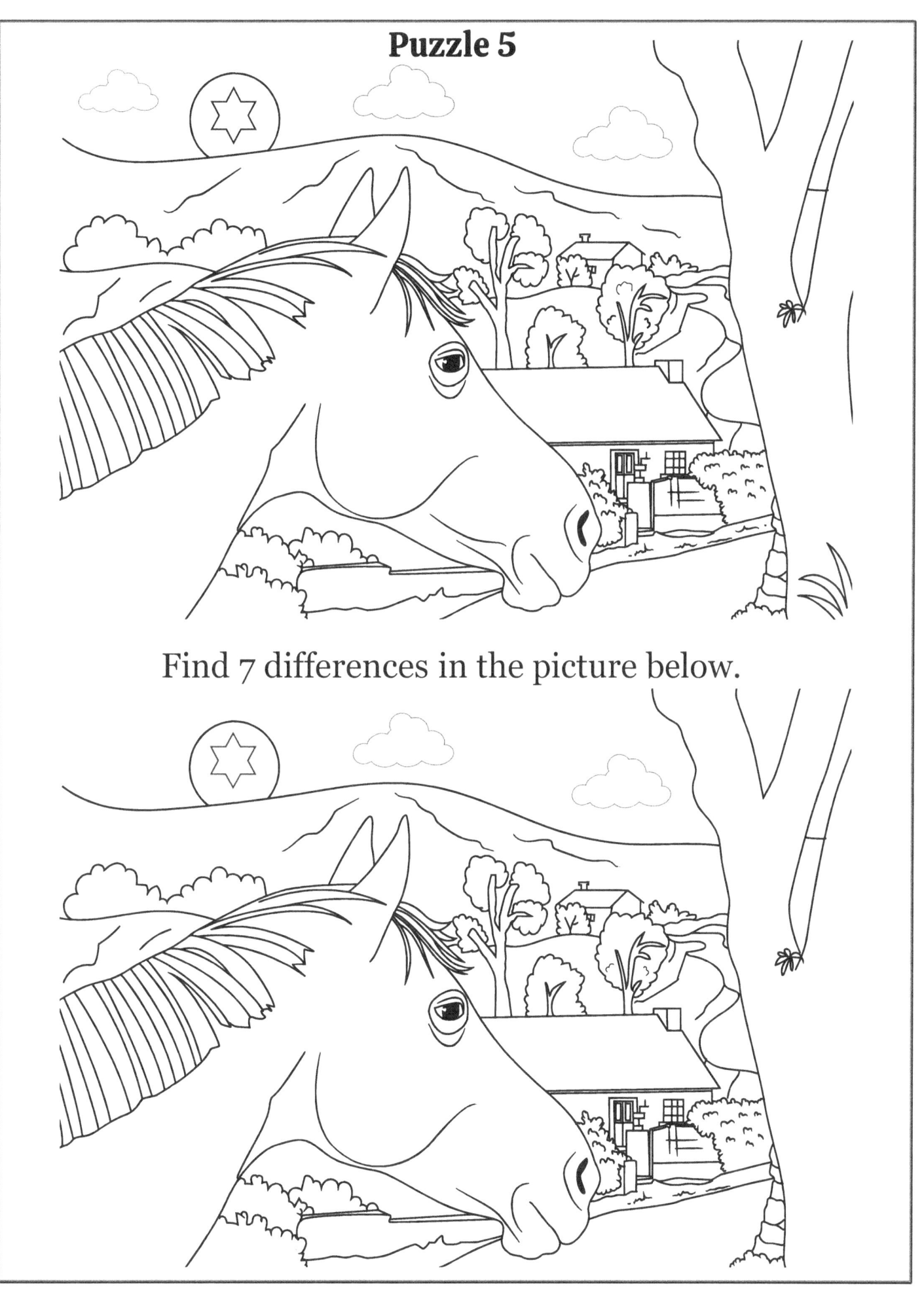

Find 7 differences in the picture below.

Puzzle 6

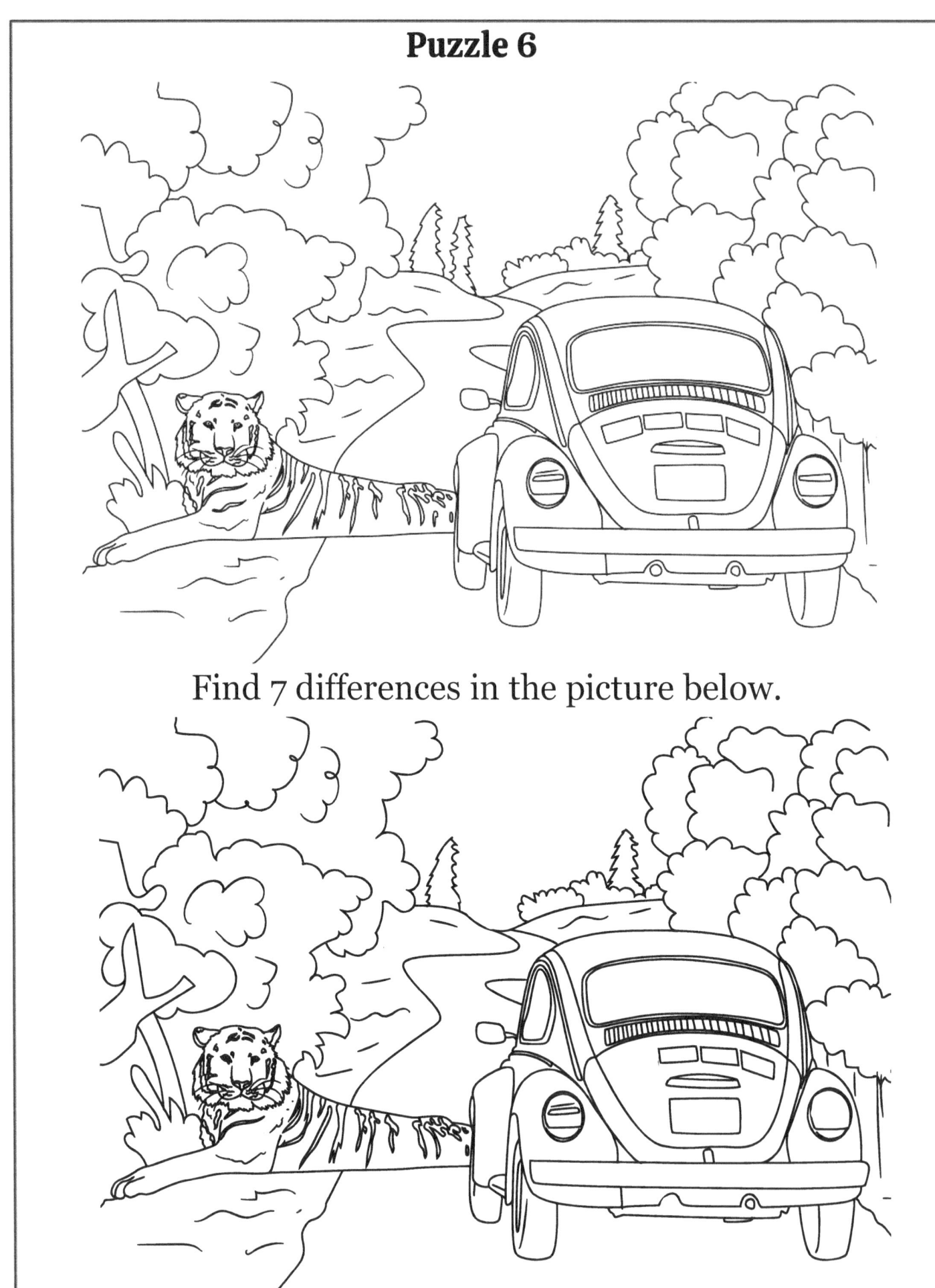

Find 7 differences in the picture below.

Puzzle 7

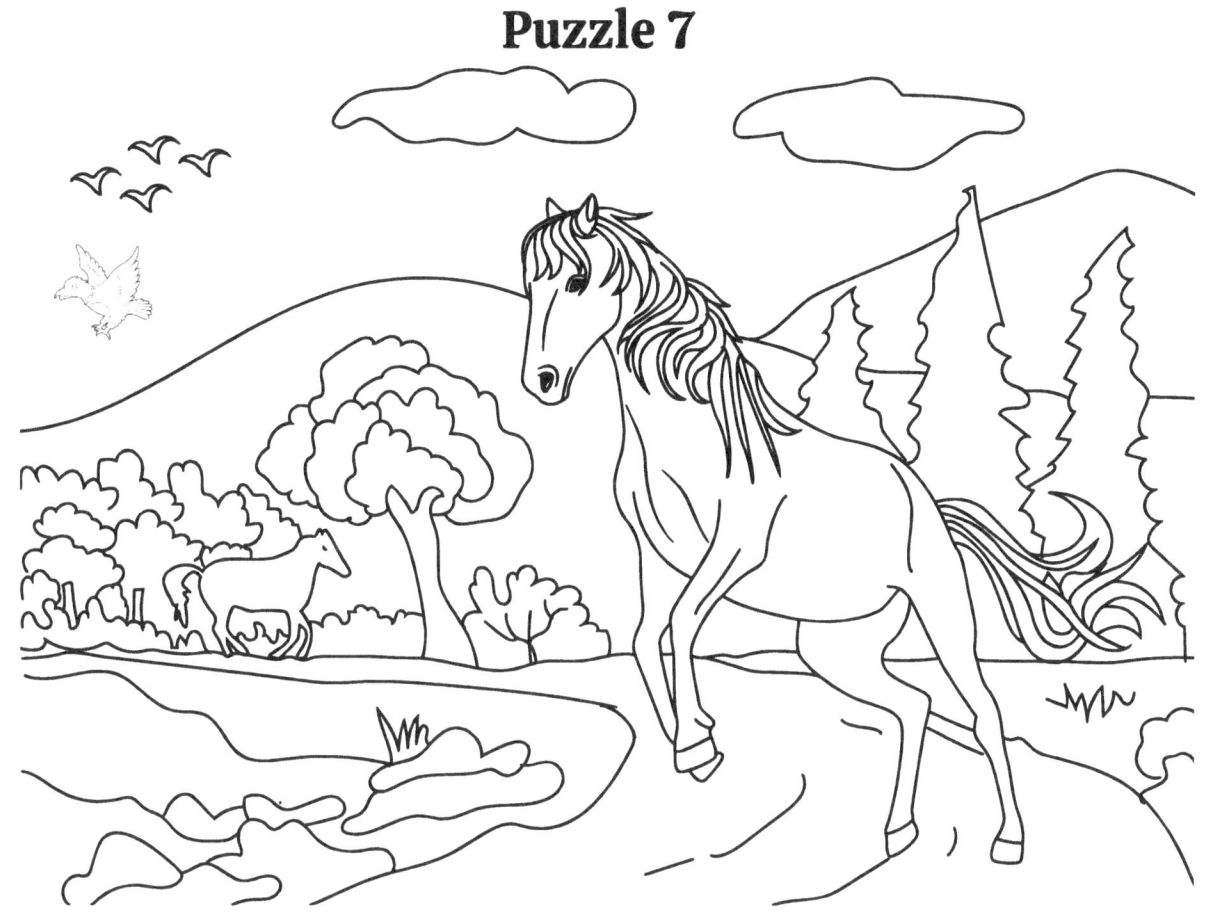

Find 4 differences in the picture below.

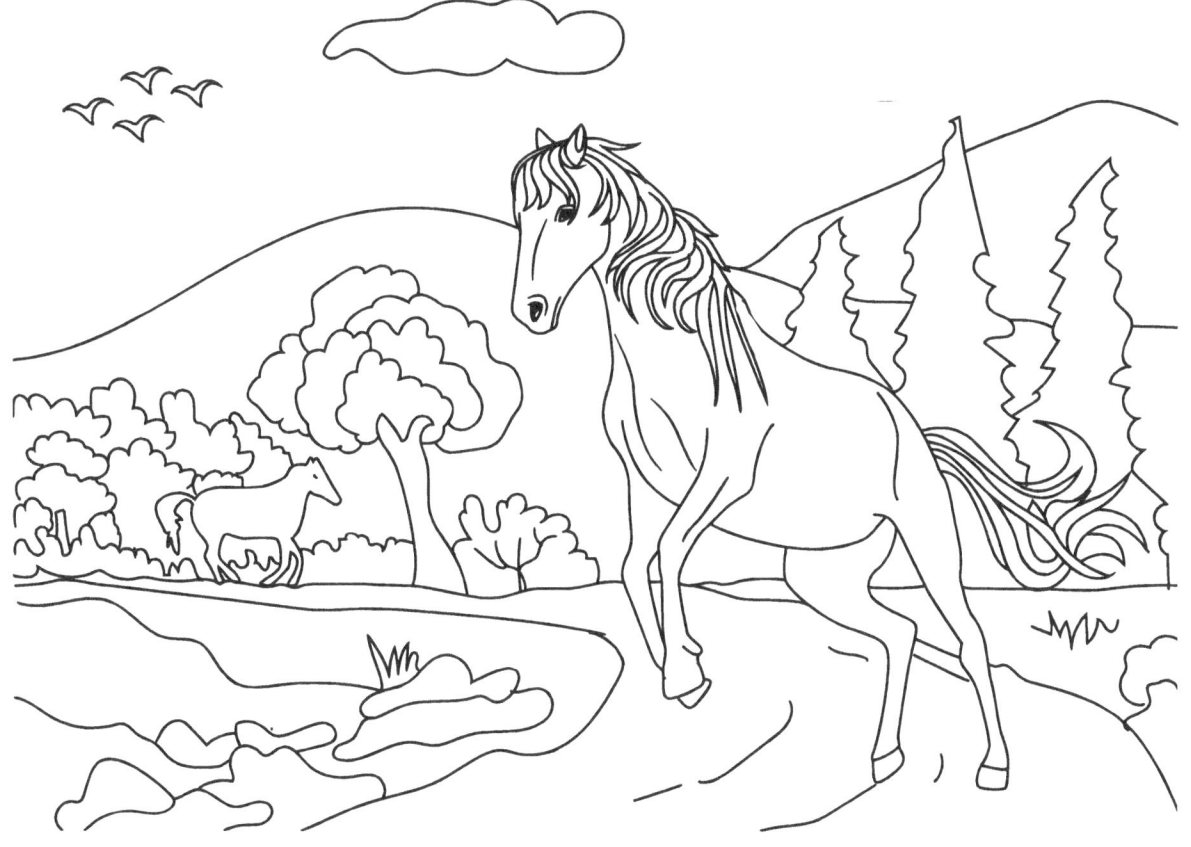

Puzzle 8

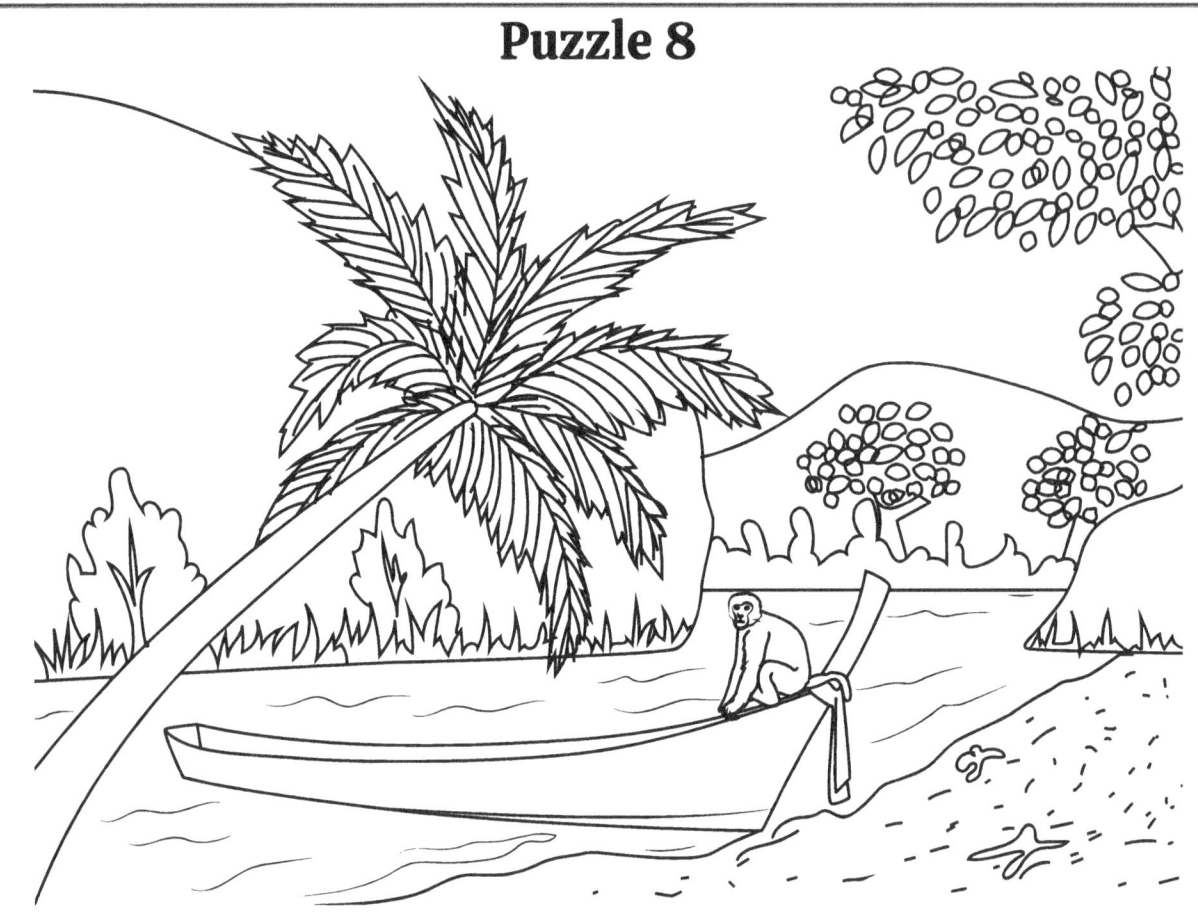

Find 8 differences in the picture below.

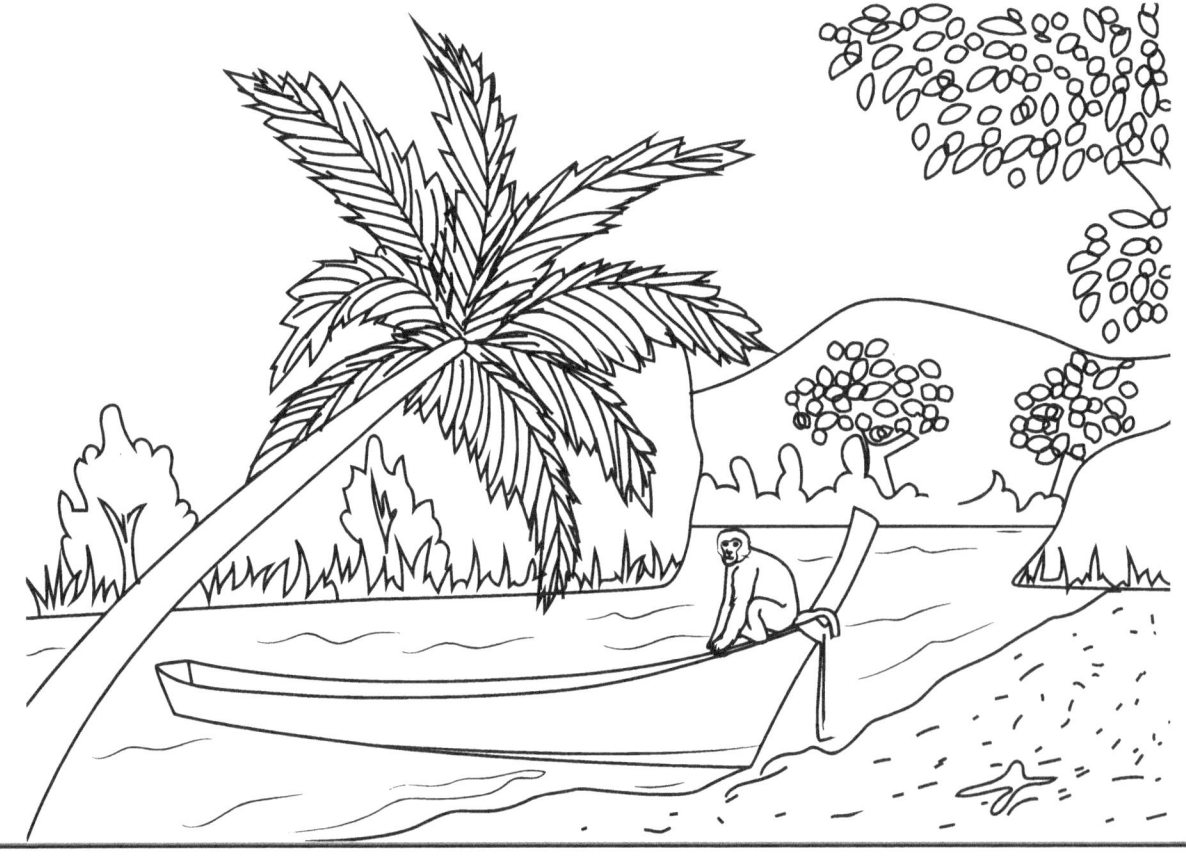

Puzzle 9

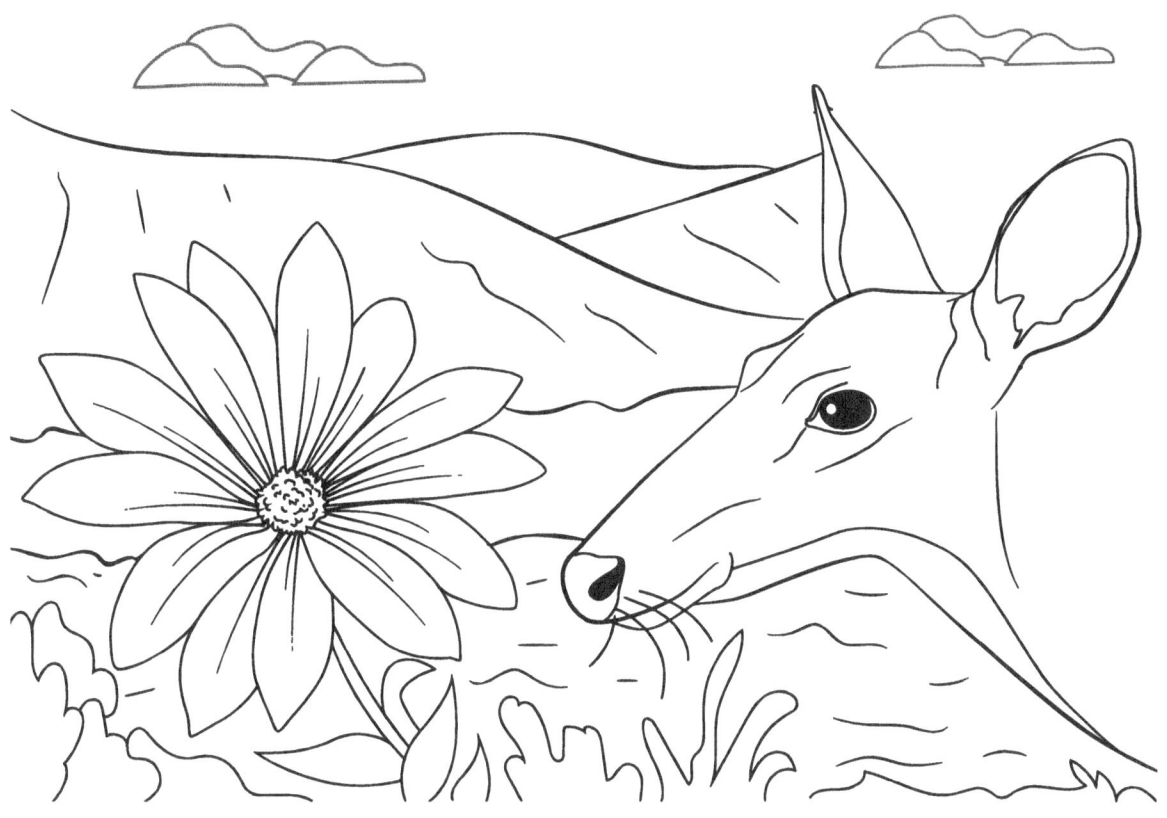

Find 6 differences in the picture below.

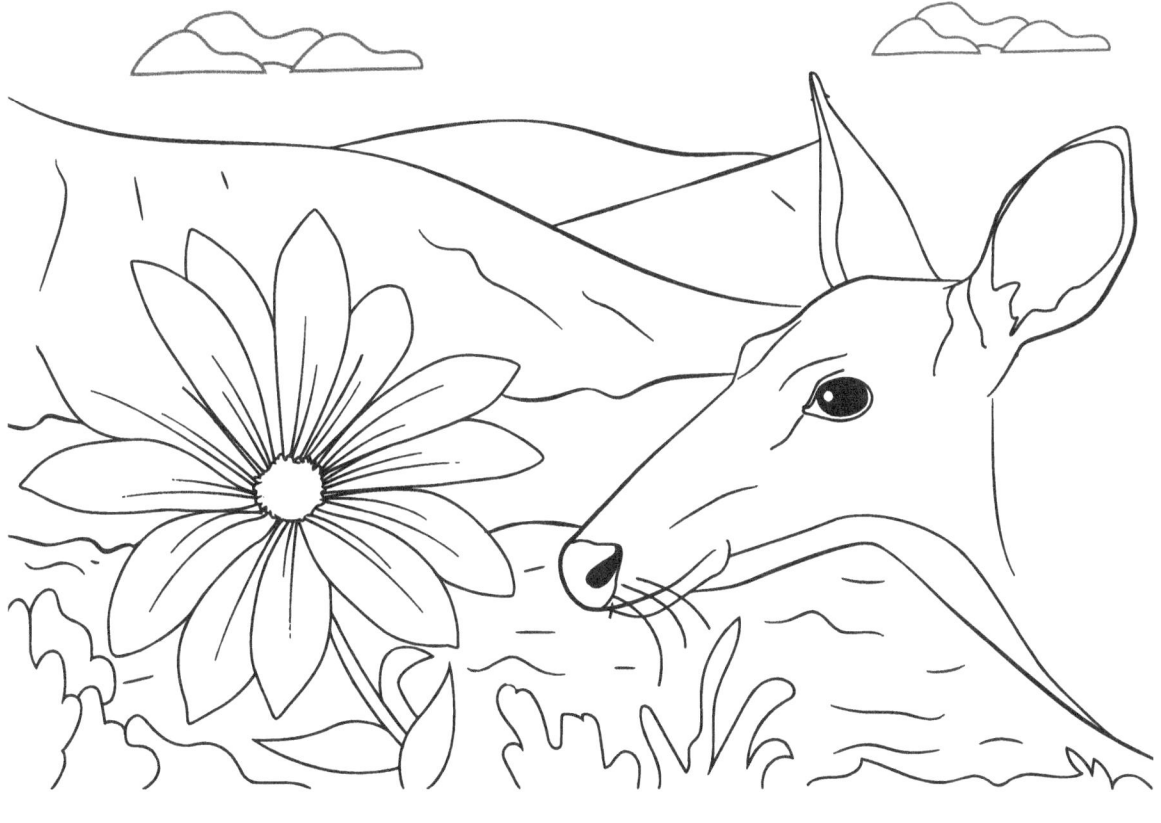

Puzzle 10

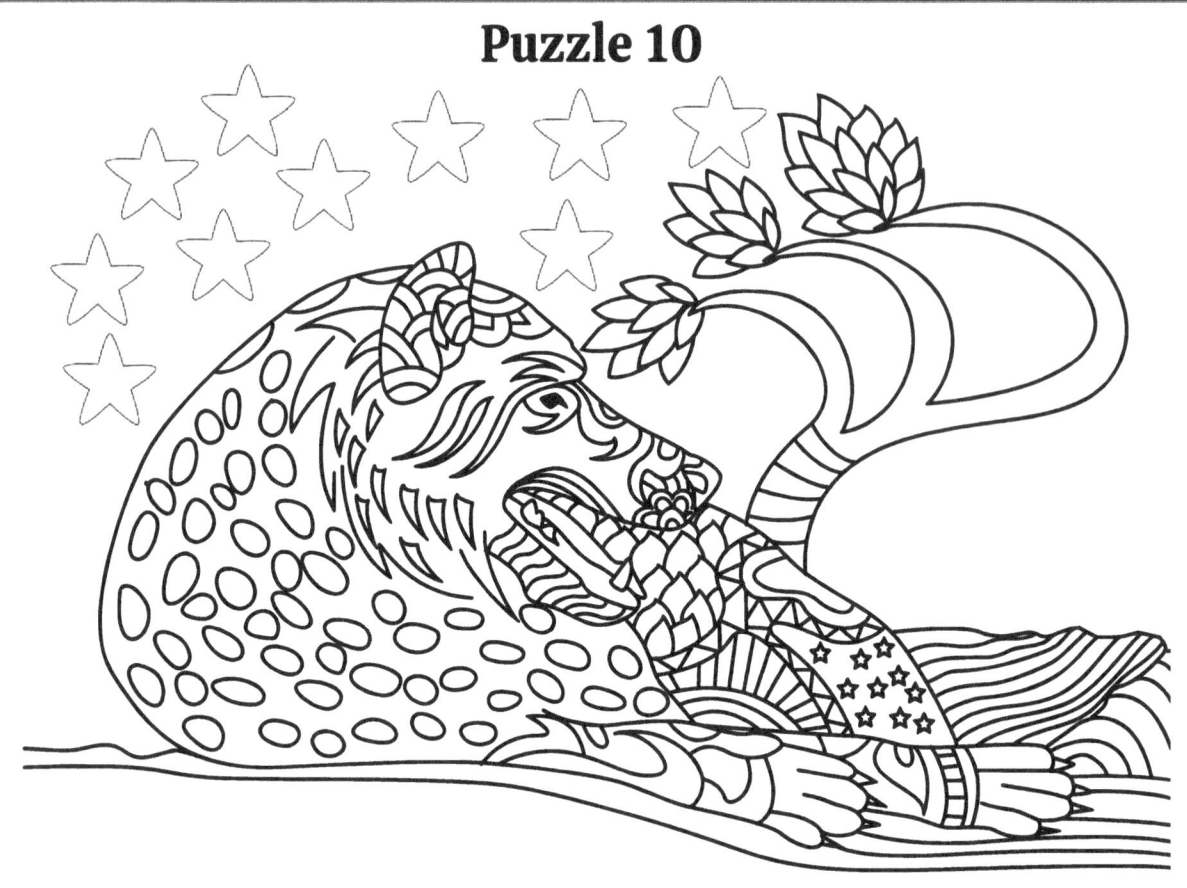

Find 8 differences in the picture below.

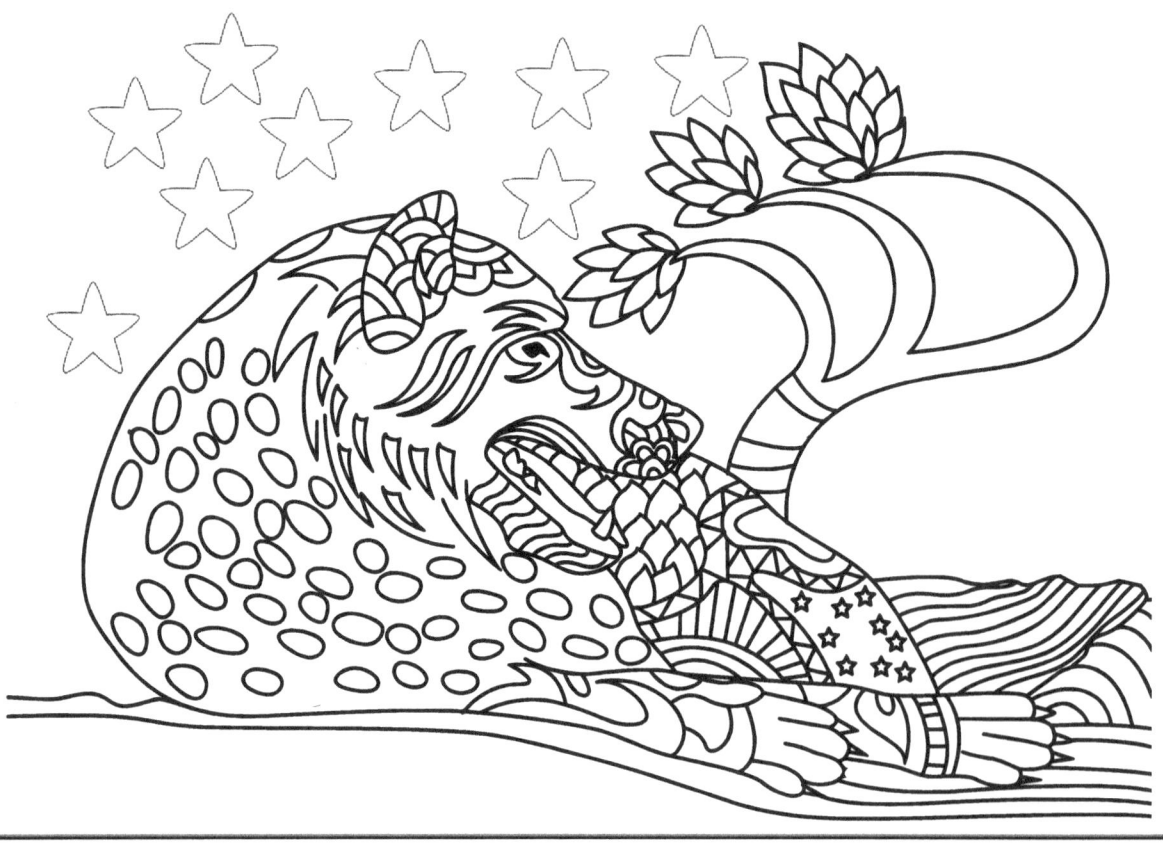

Puzzle 11

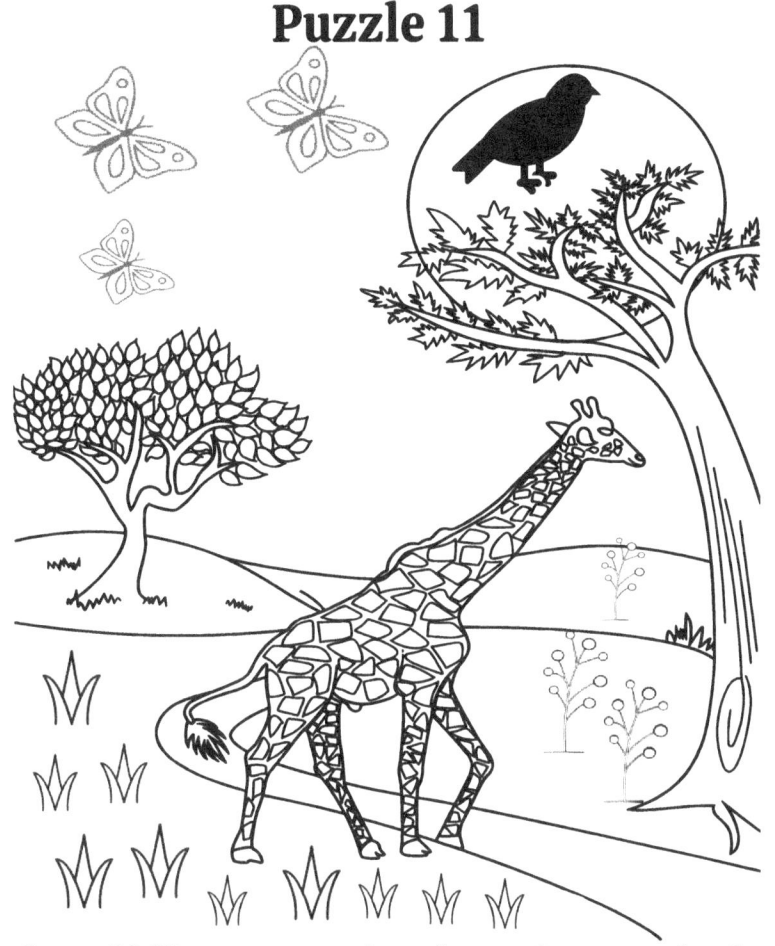

Find 9 differences in the picture below.

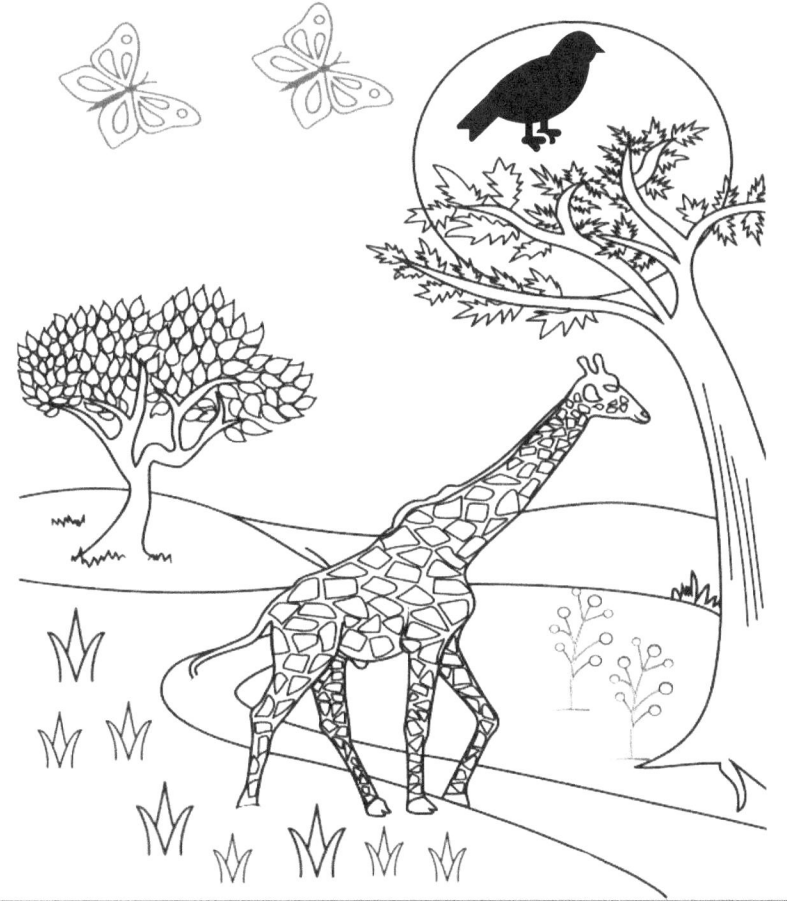

Puzzle 12

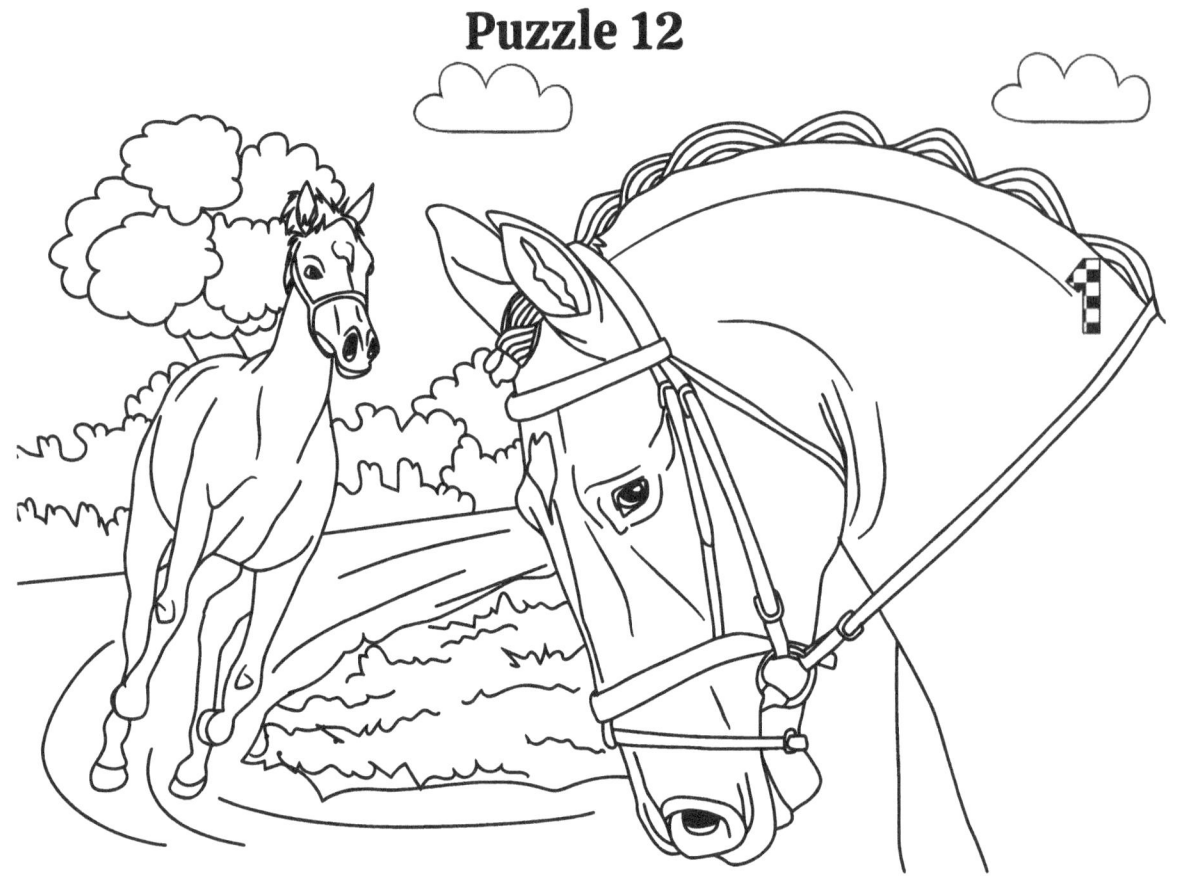

Find 2 differences in the picture below.

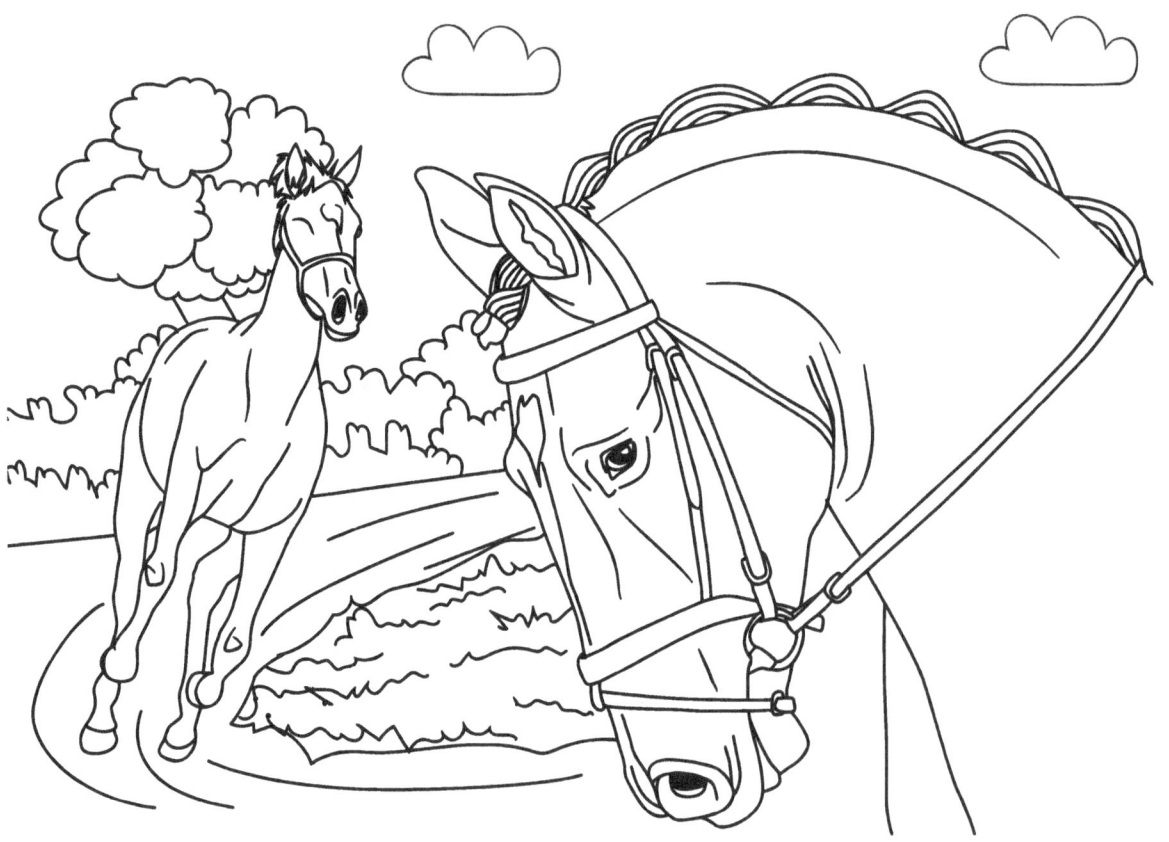

Puzzle 13

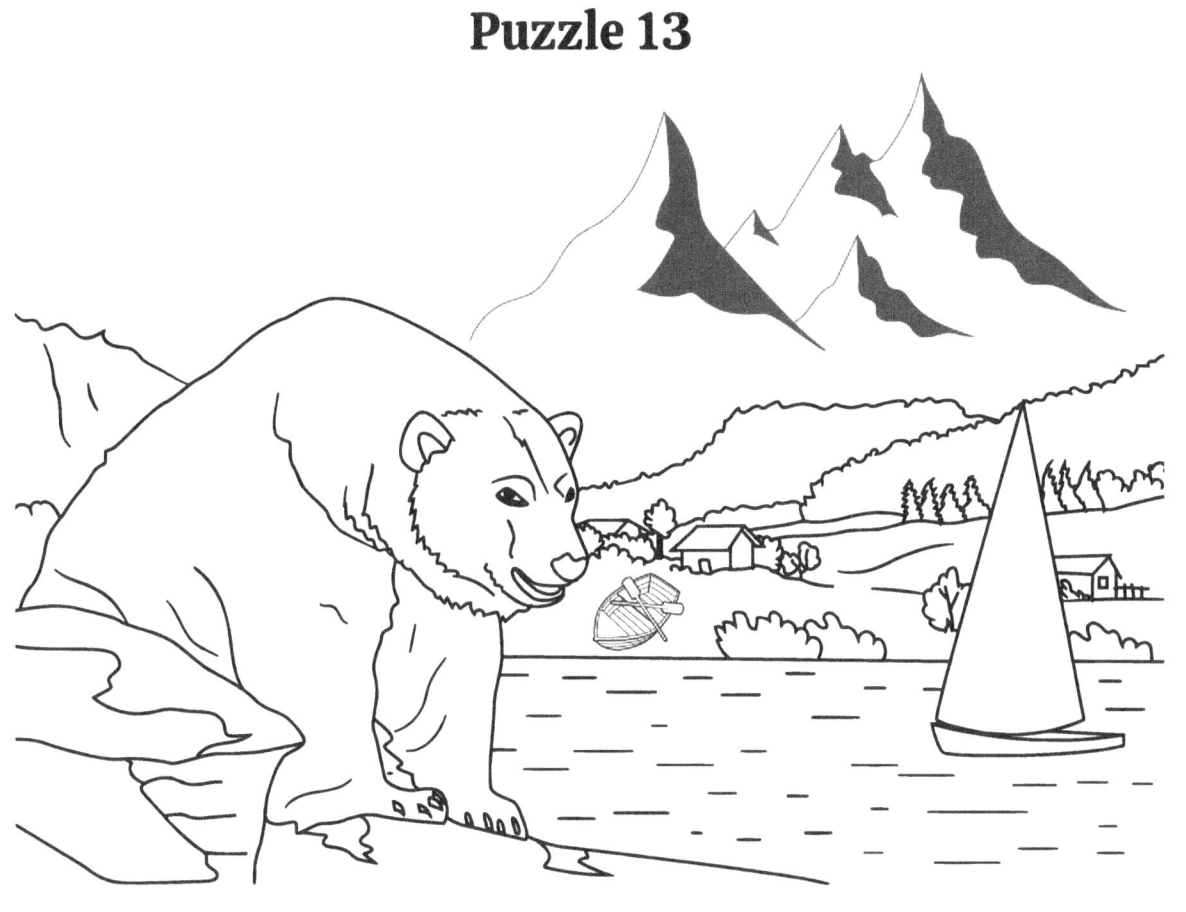

Find 1 difference in the picture below.

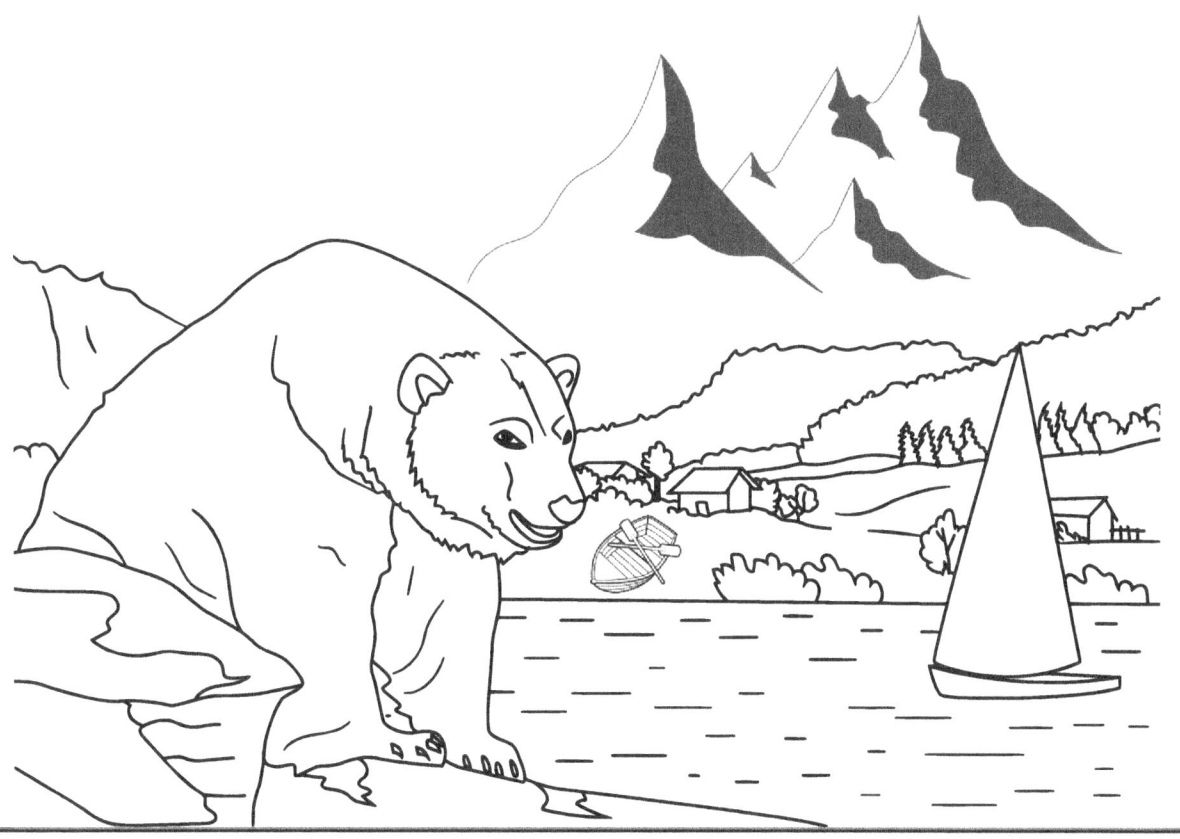

Puzzle 14

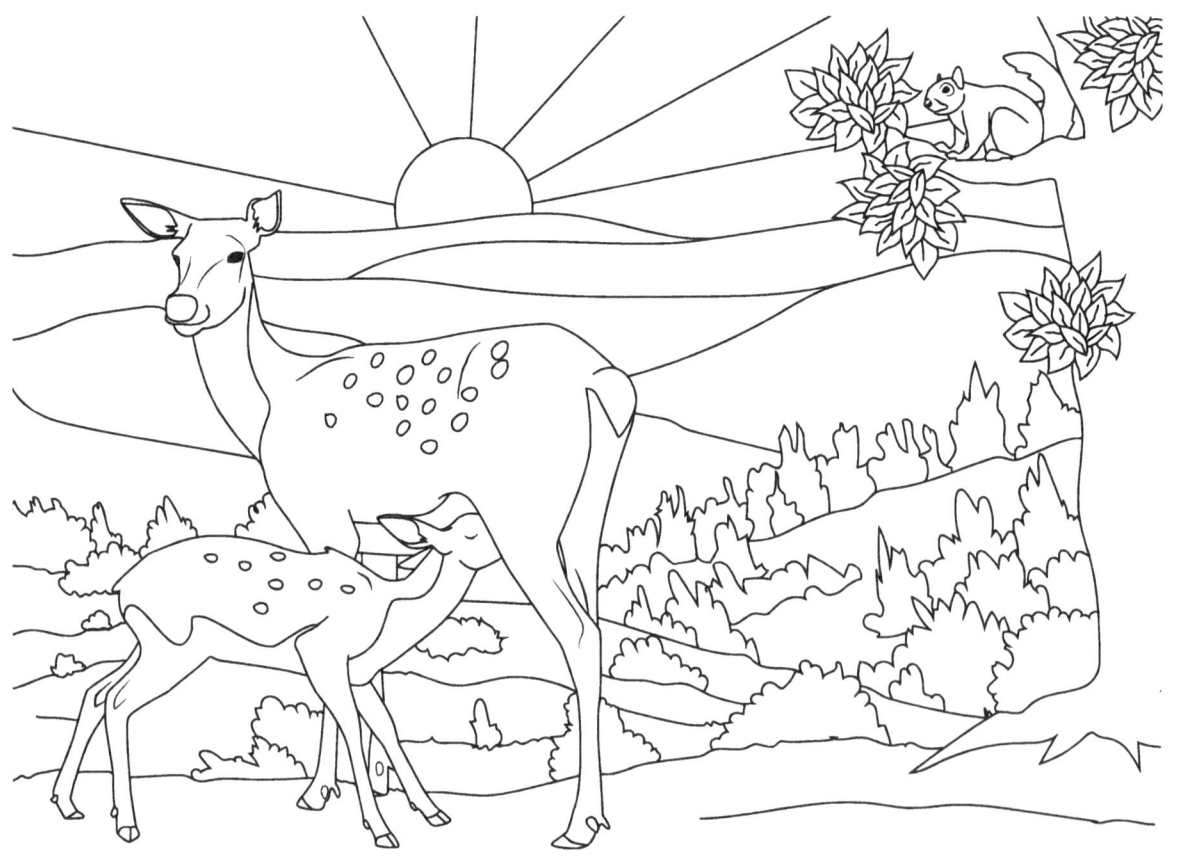

Find 5 differences in the picture below.

Puzzle 15

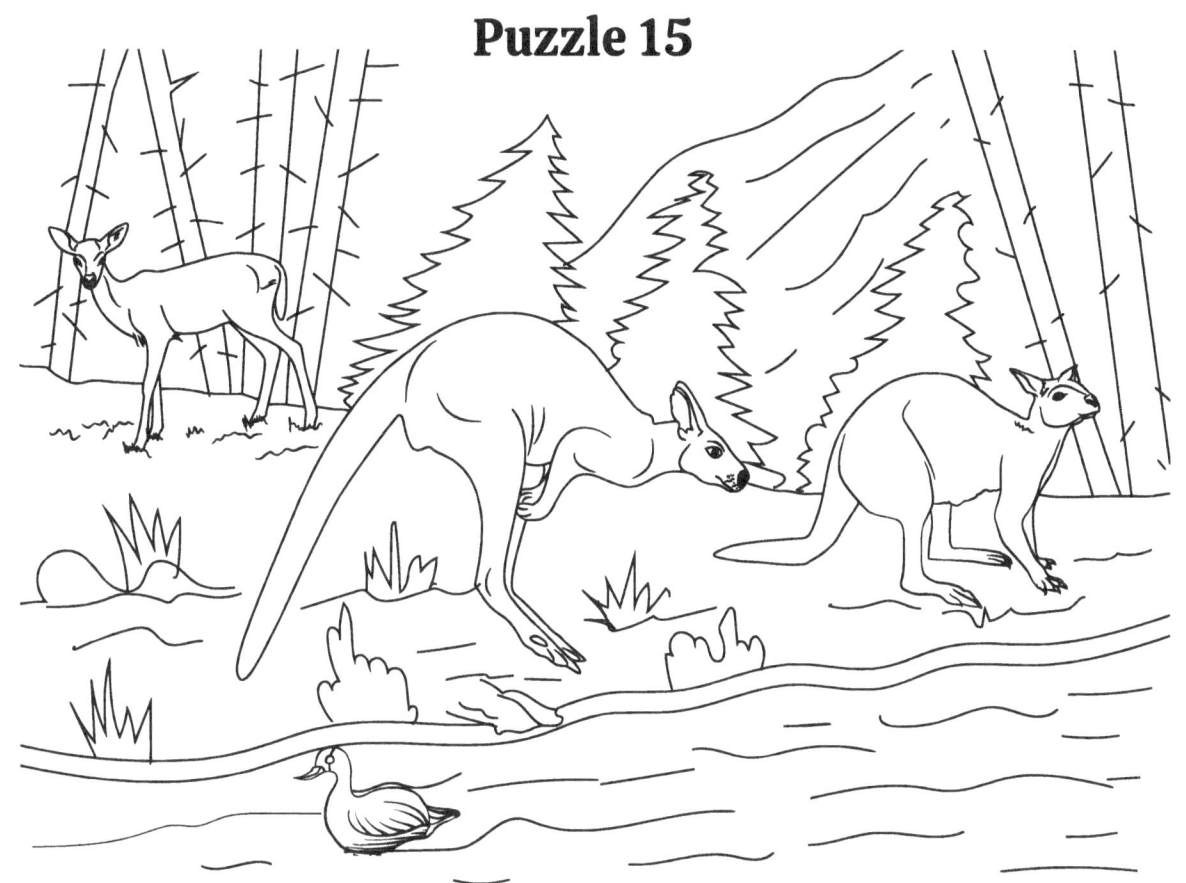

Find 5 differences in the picture below.

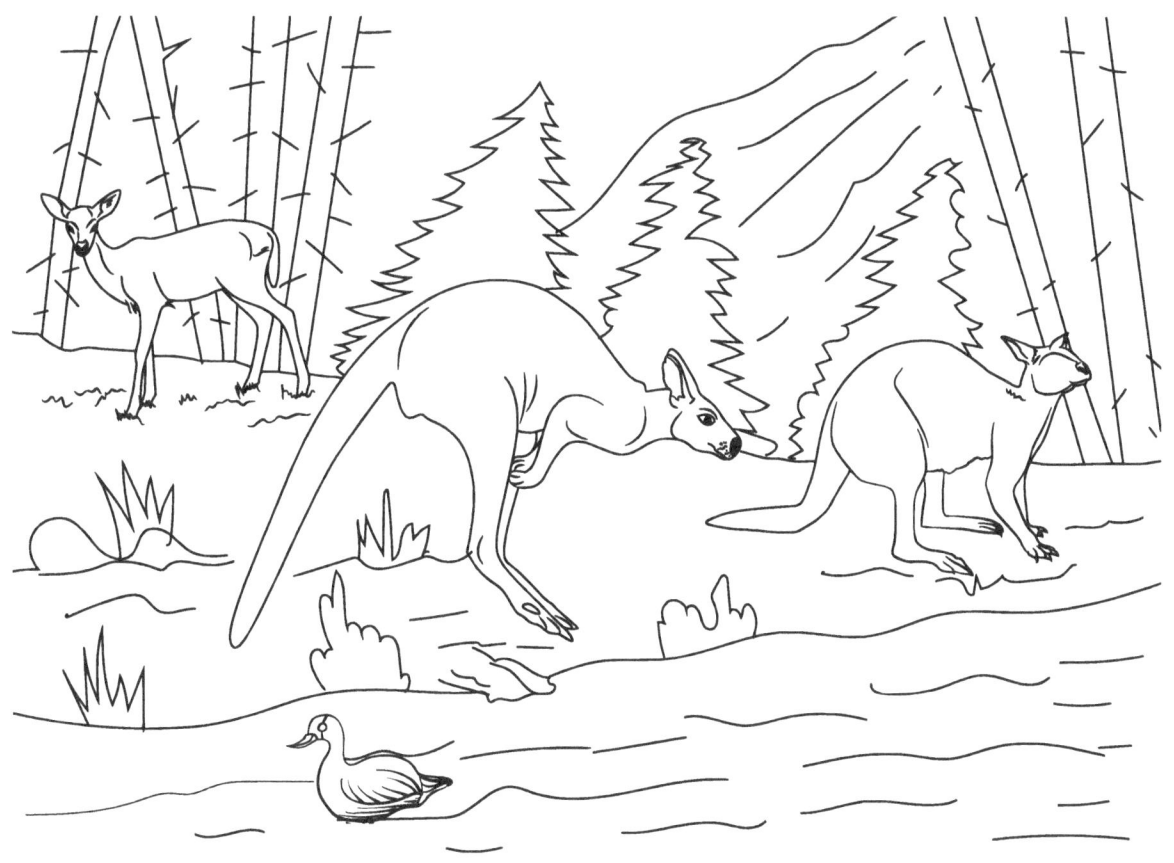

Puzzle 16

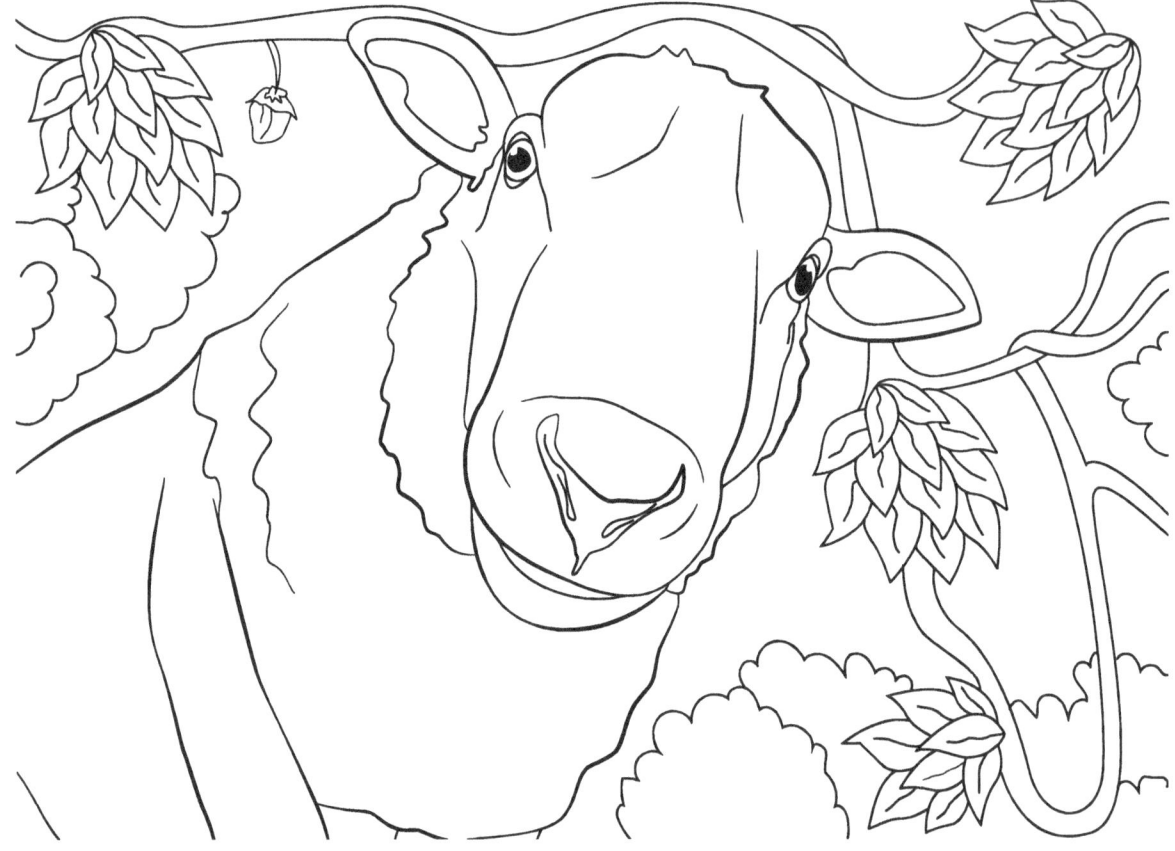

Find 2 differences in the picture below.

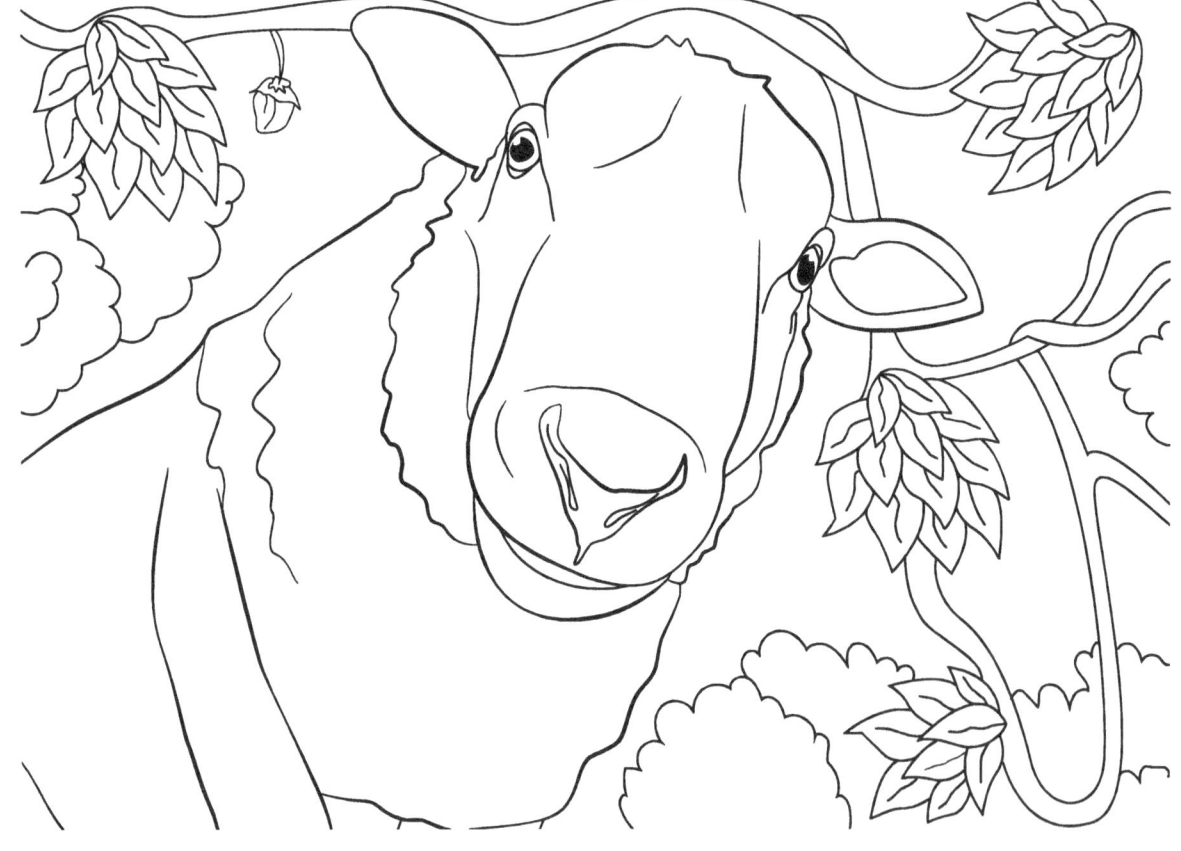

Puzzle 17

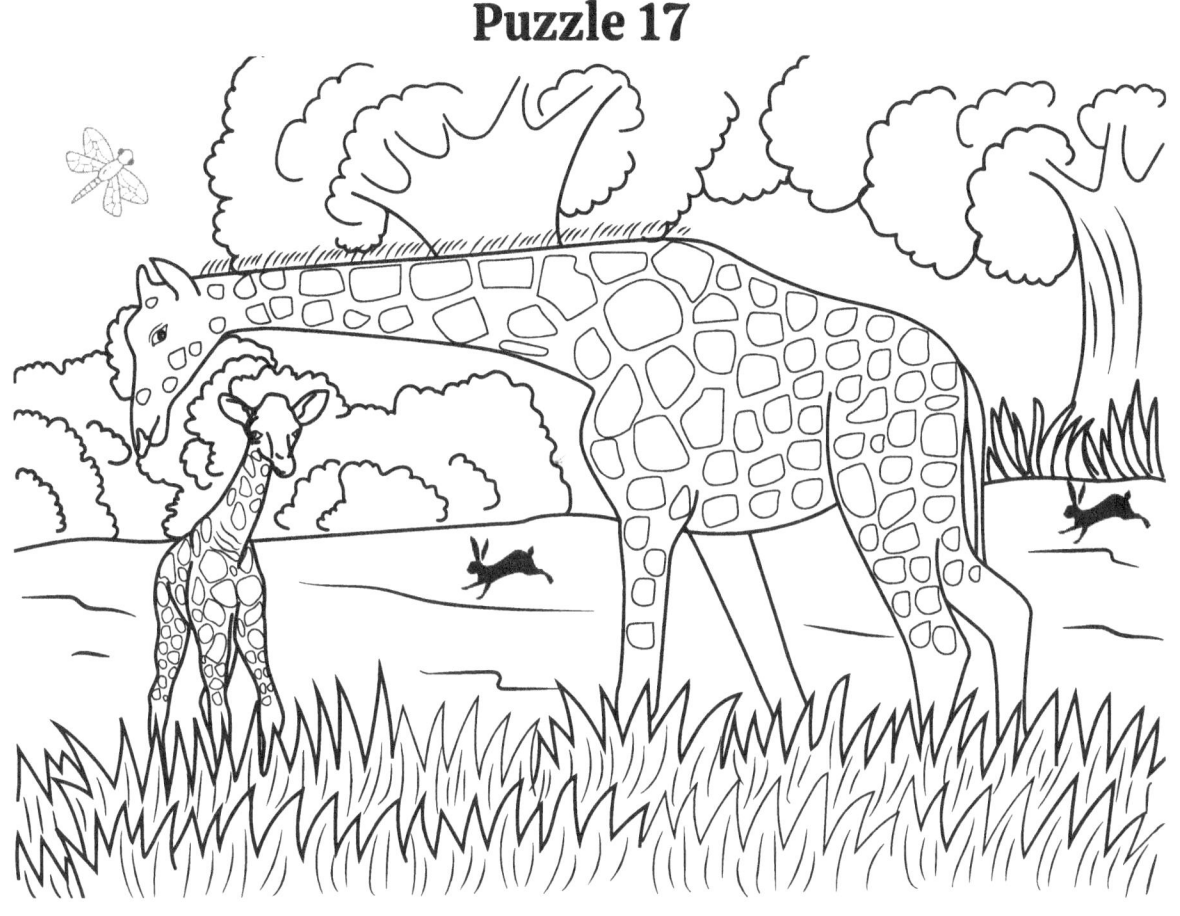

Find 8 differences in the picture below.

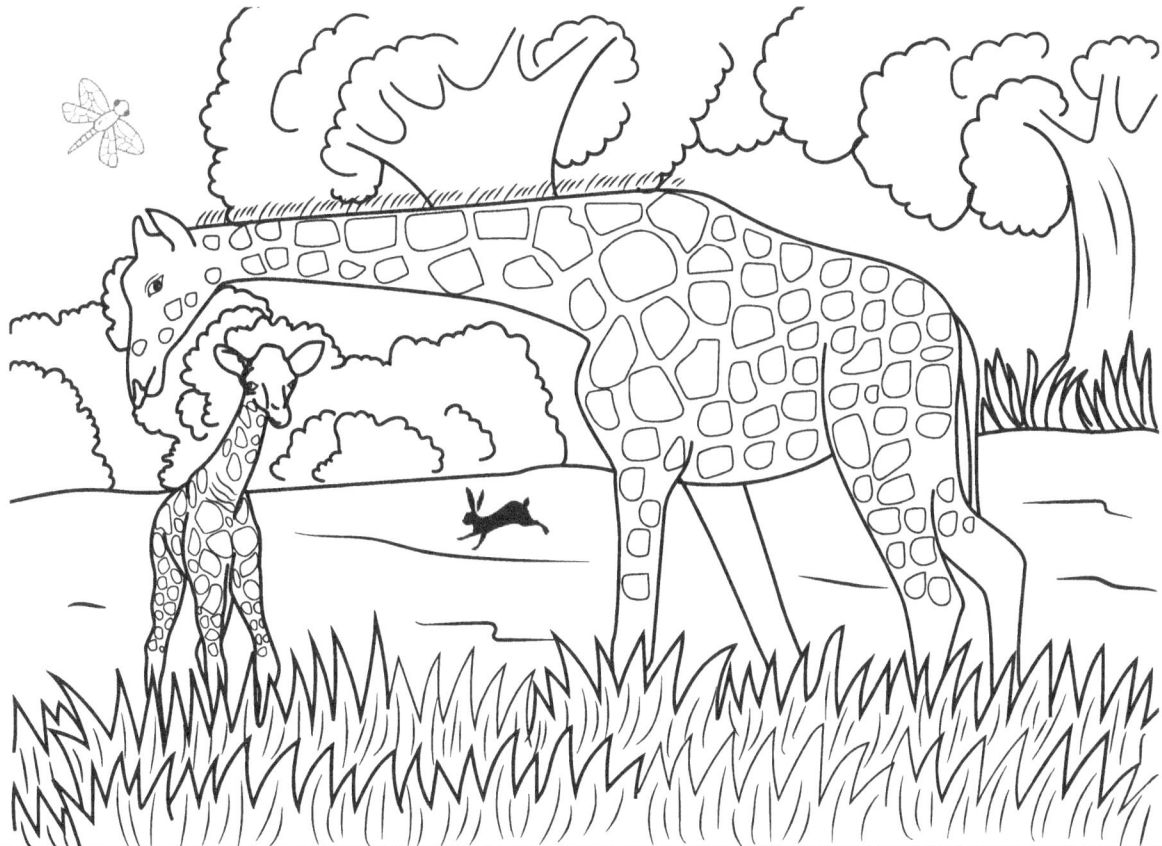

Puzzle 18

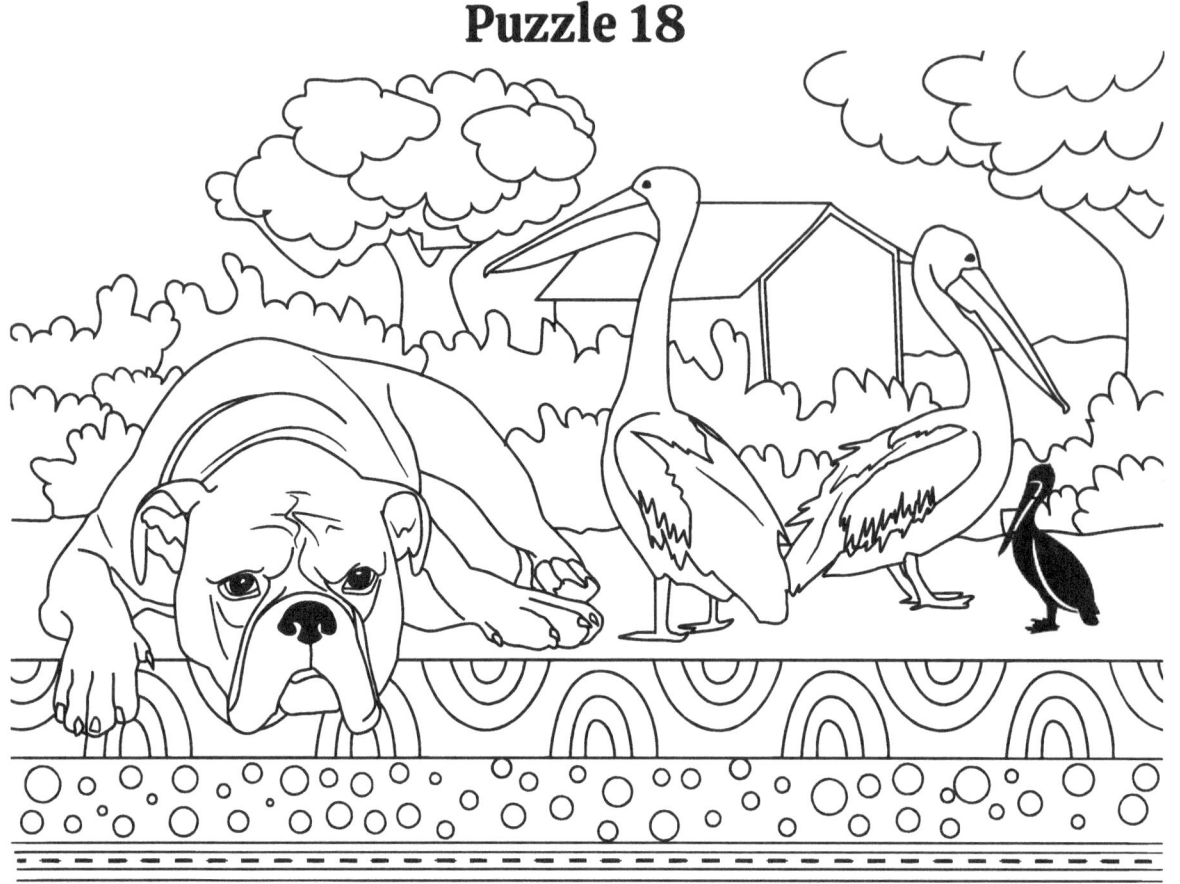

Find 10 differences in the picture below.

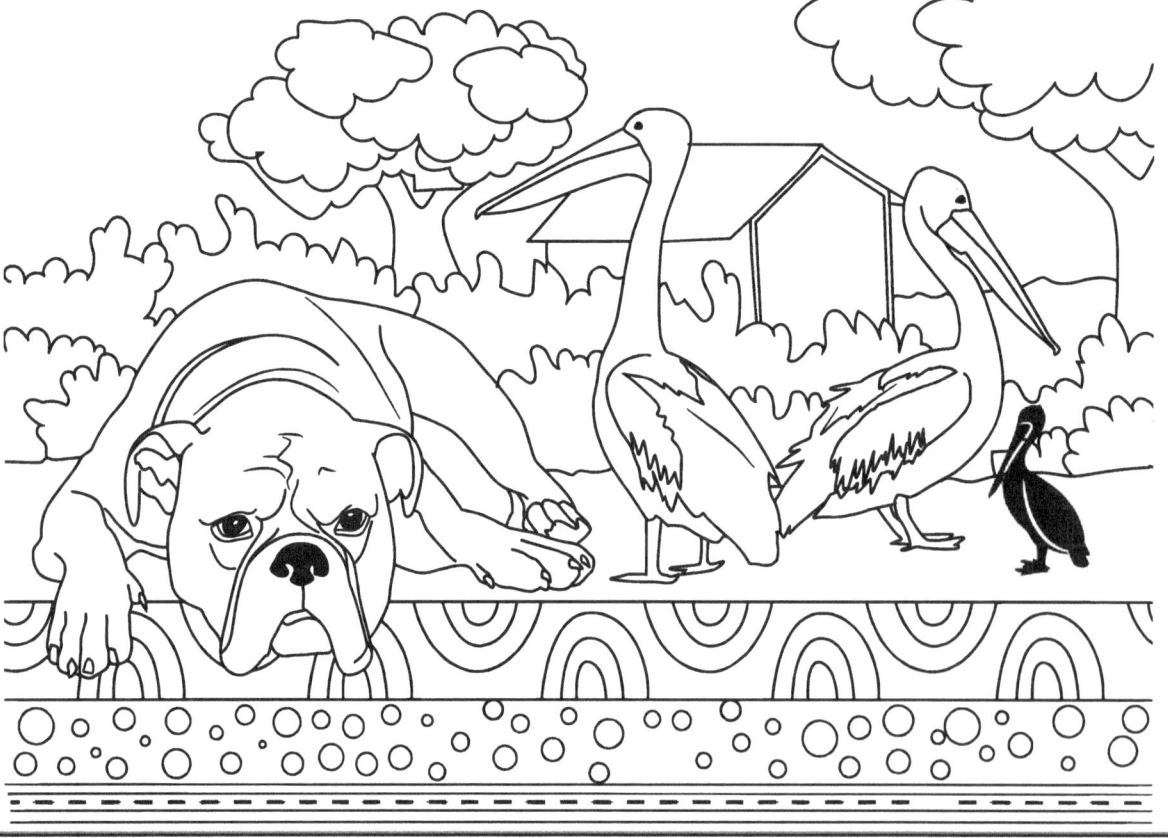

Puzzle 19

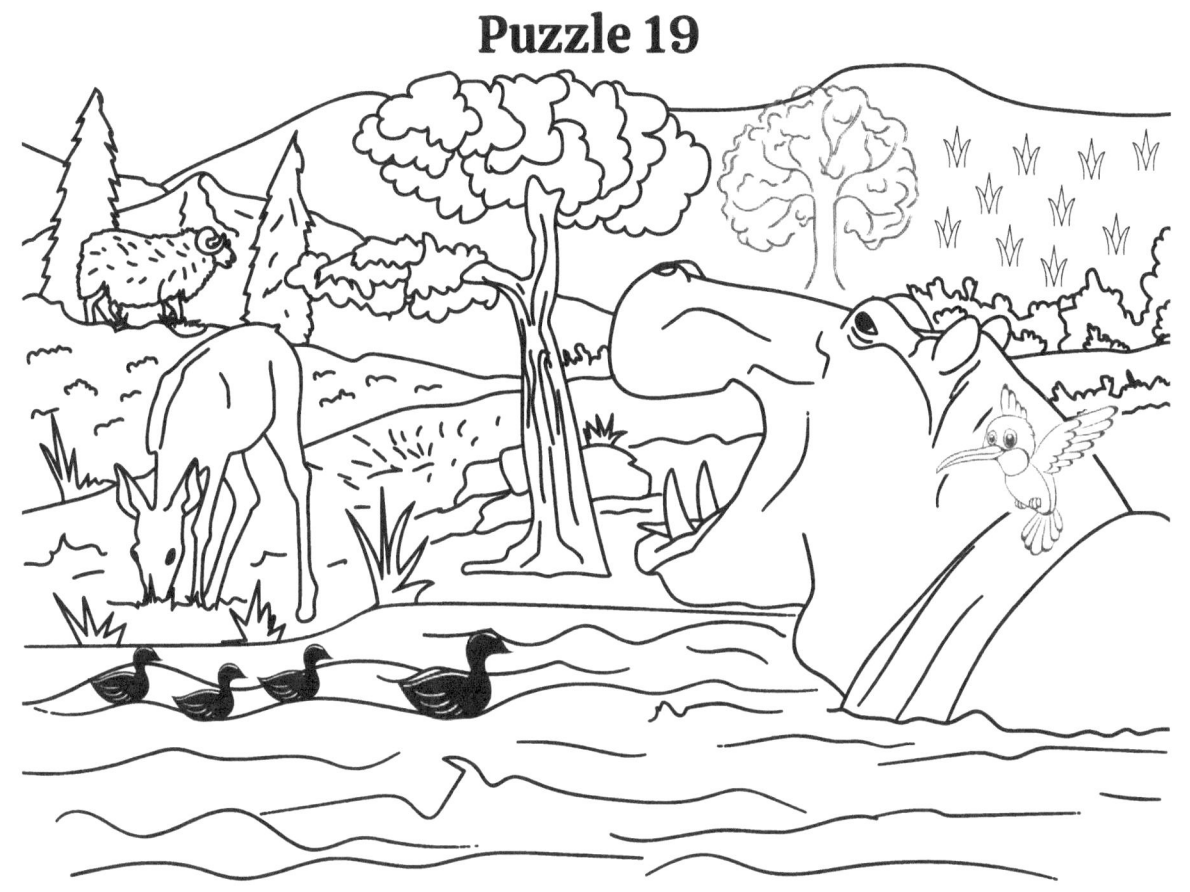

Find 10 differences in the picture below.

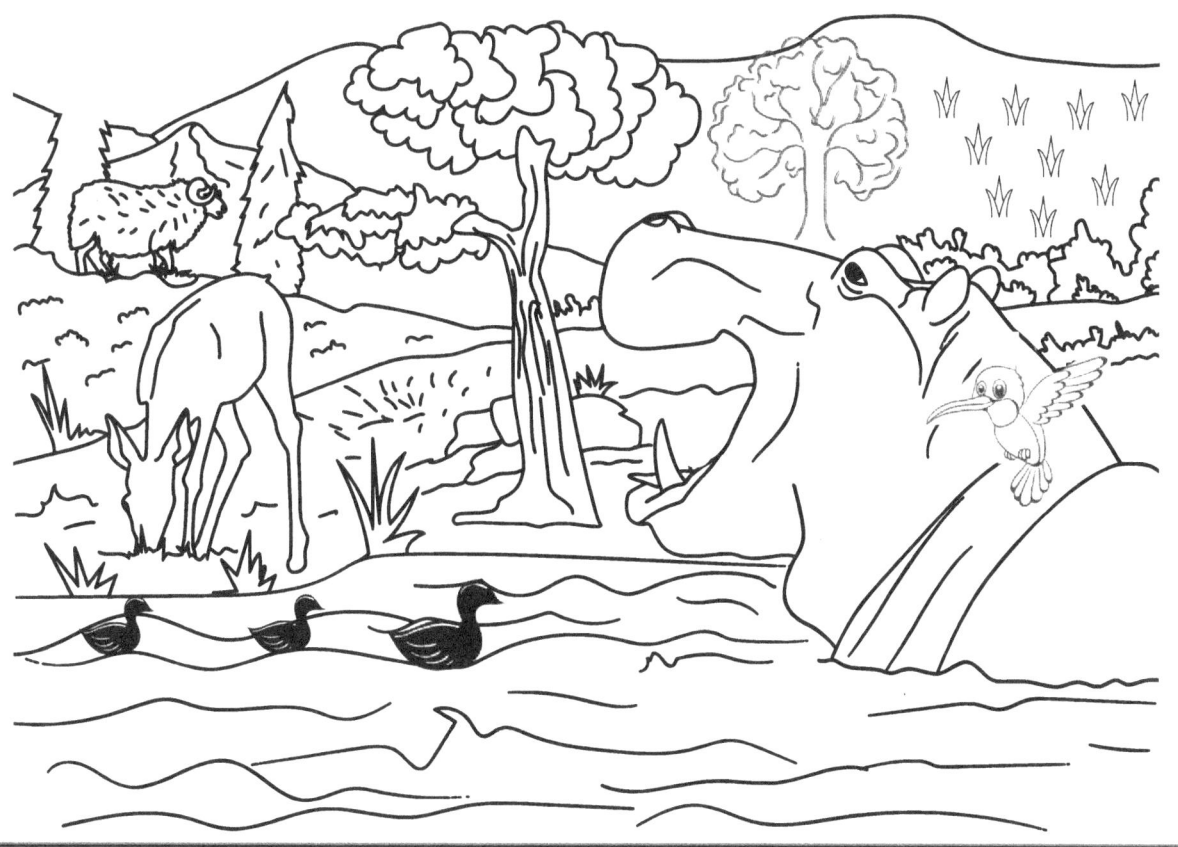

Puzzle 20

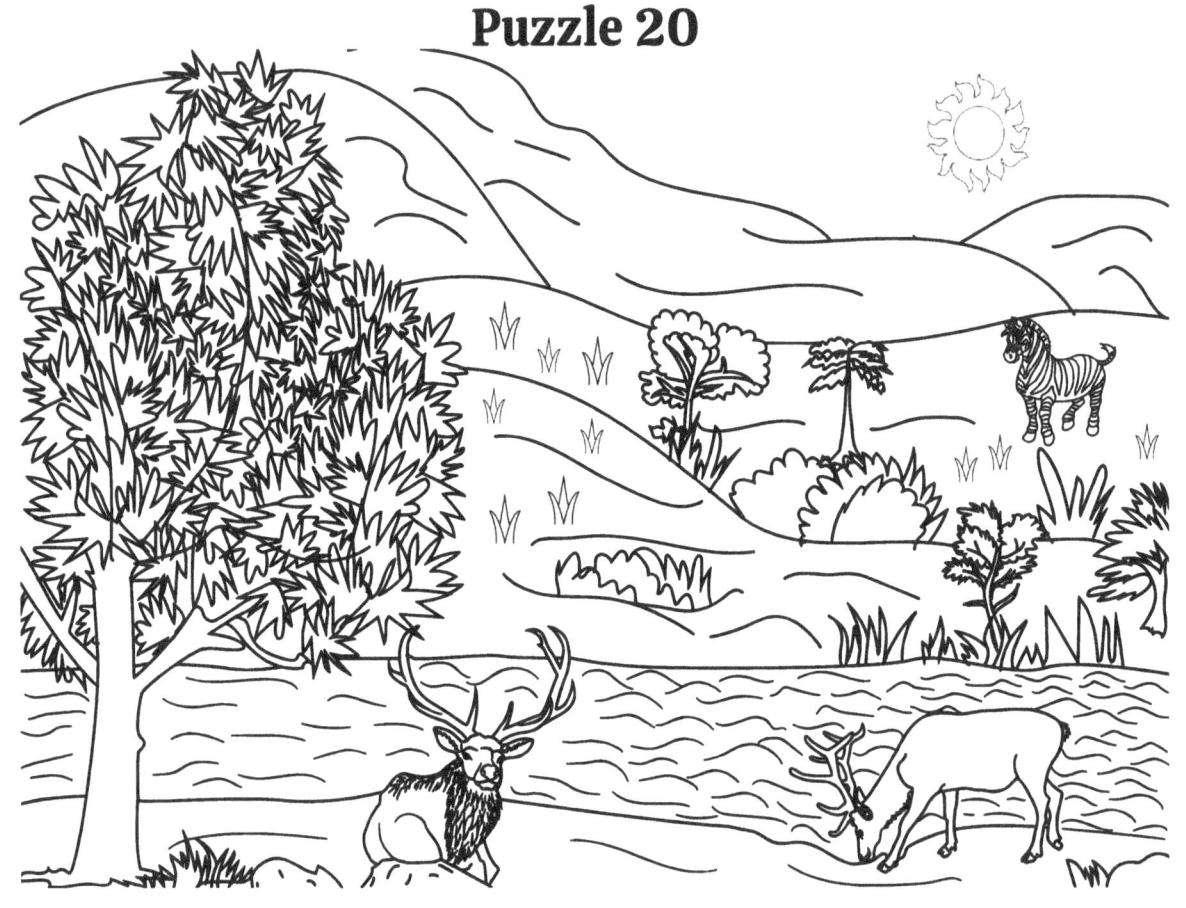

Find 5 differences in the picture below.

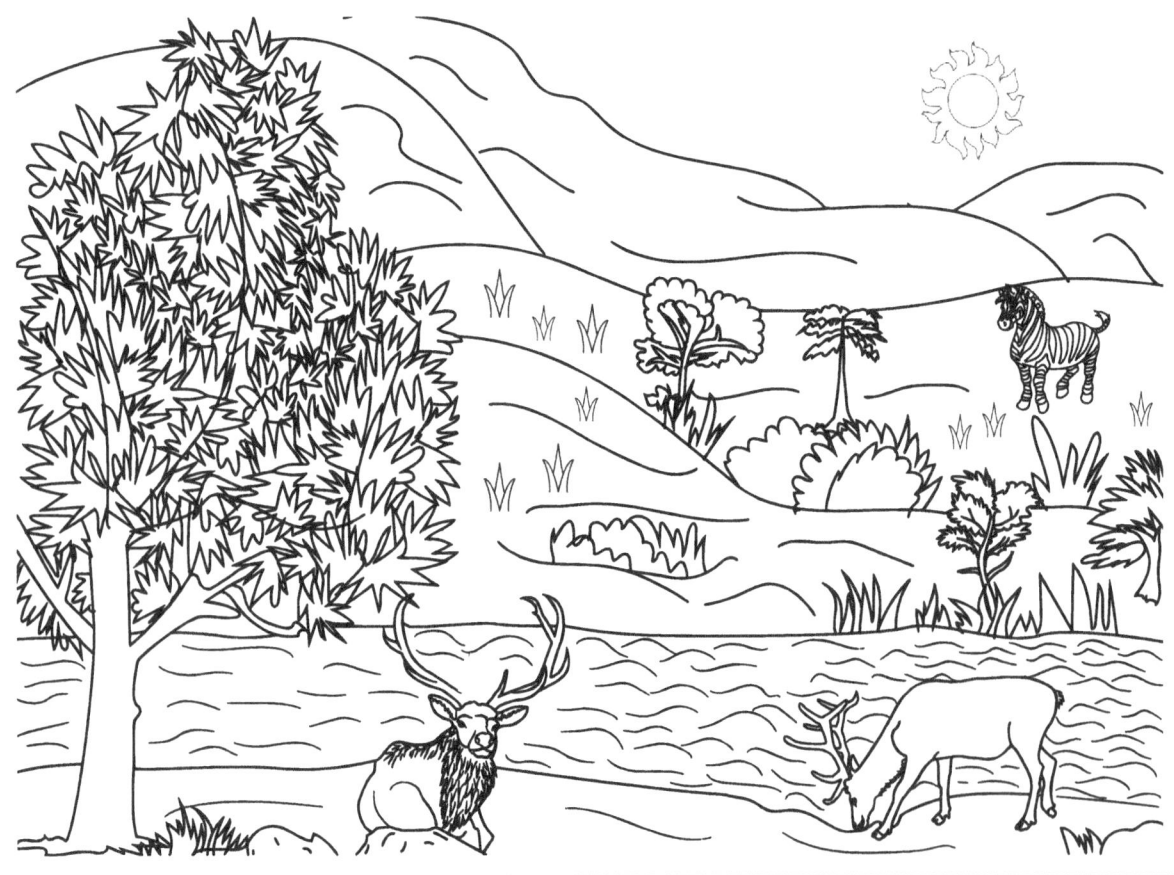

Puzzle 21

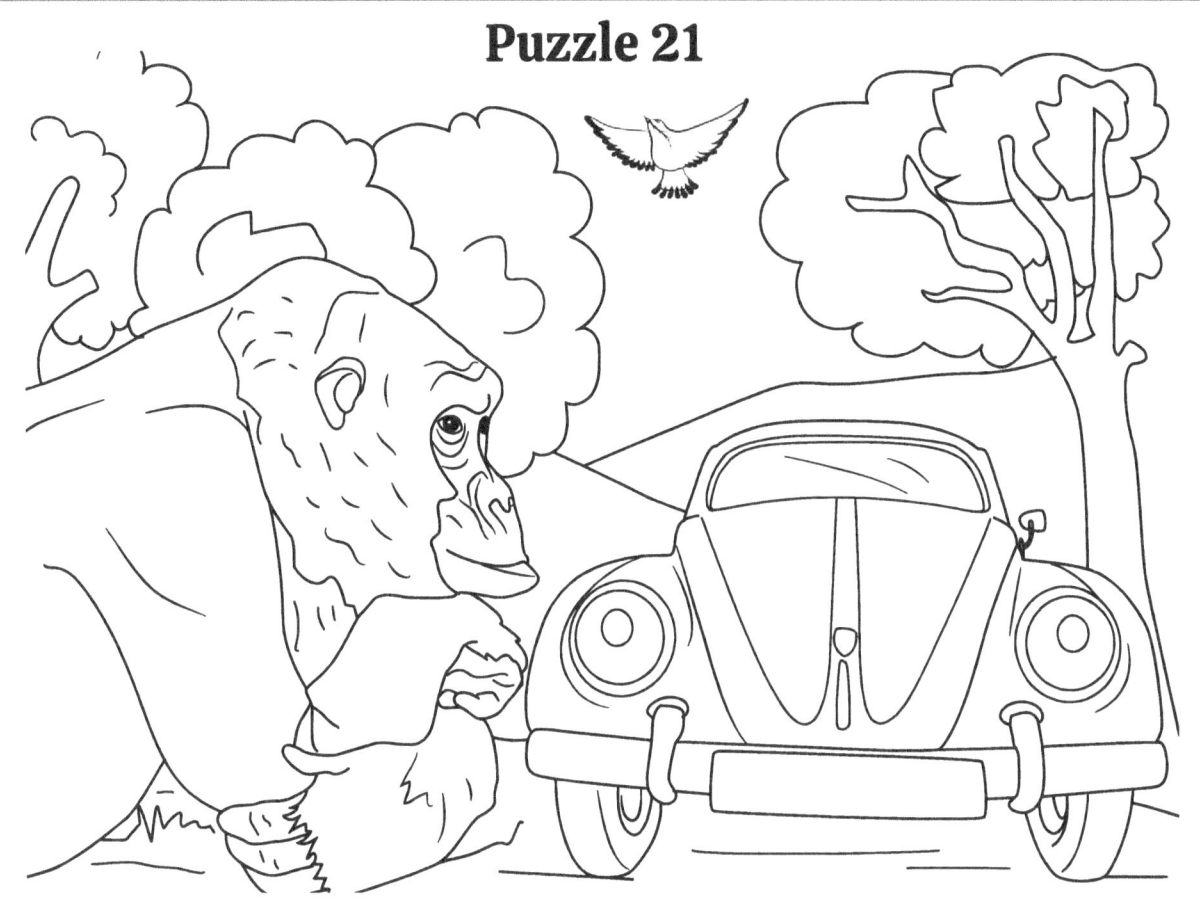

Find 3 differences in the picture below.

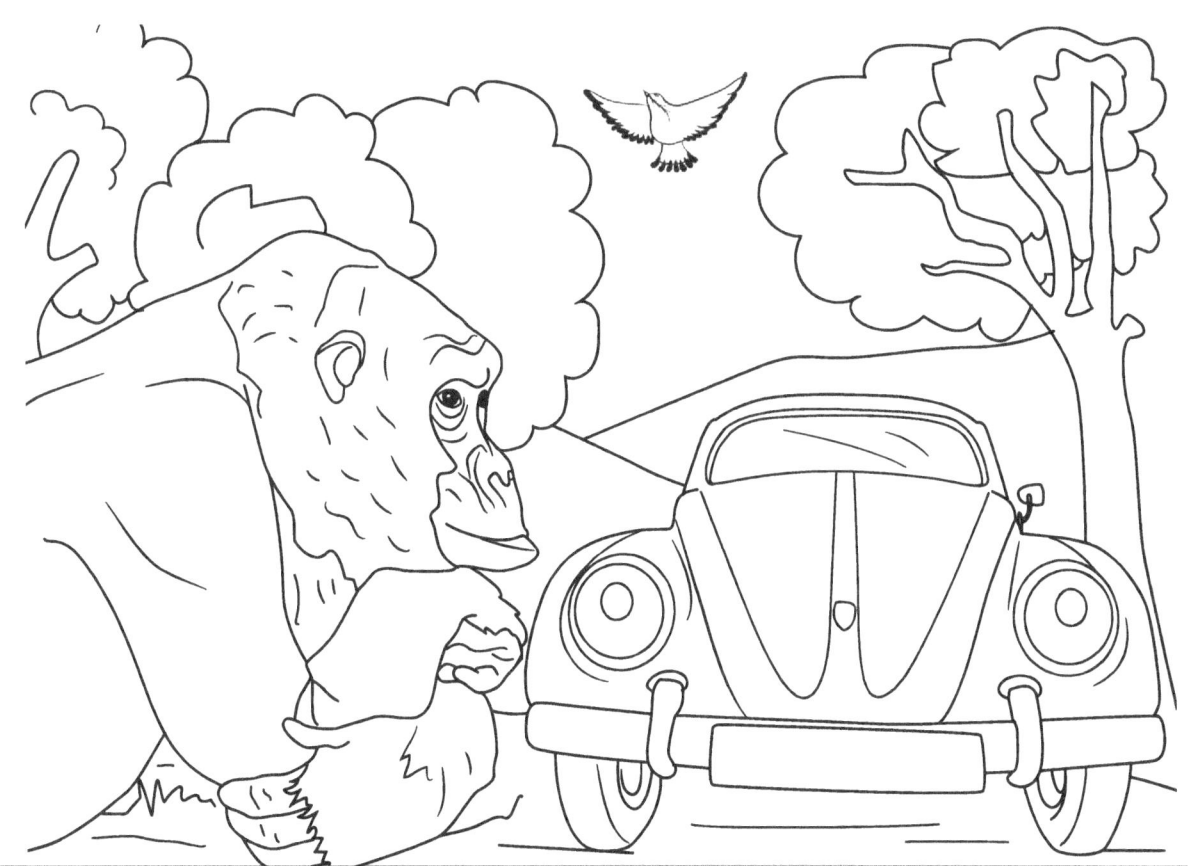

Puzzle 22

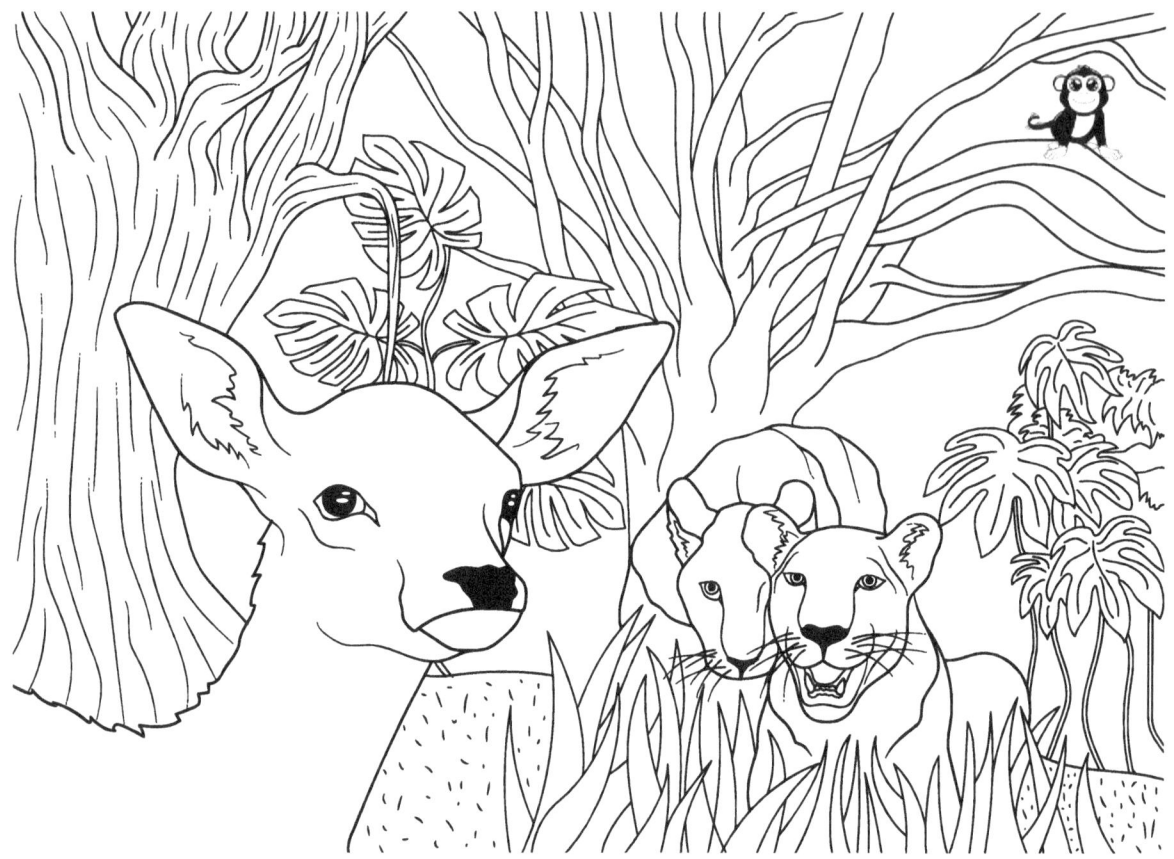

Find 4 differences in the picture below.

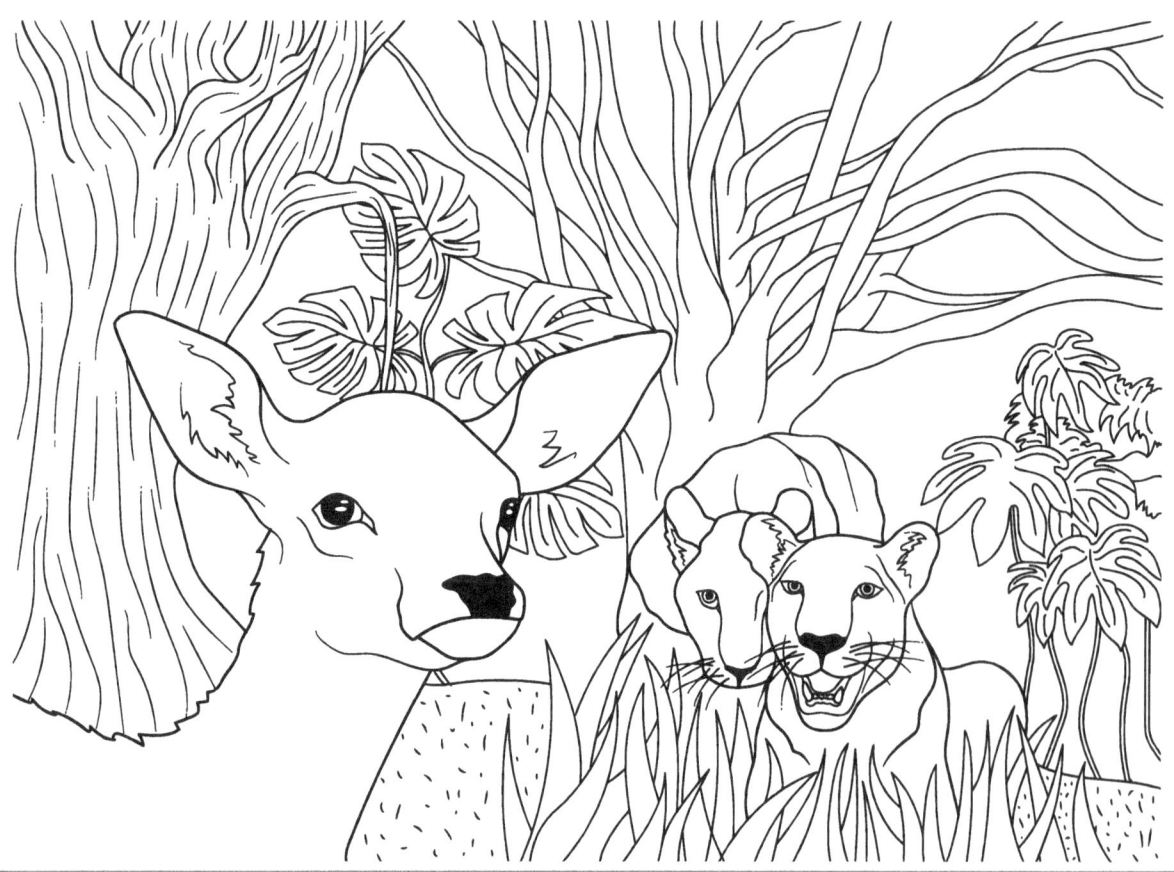

Puzzle 23

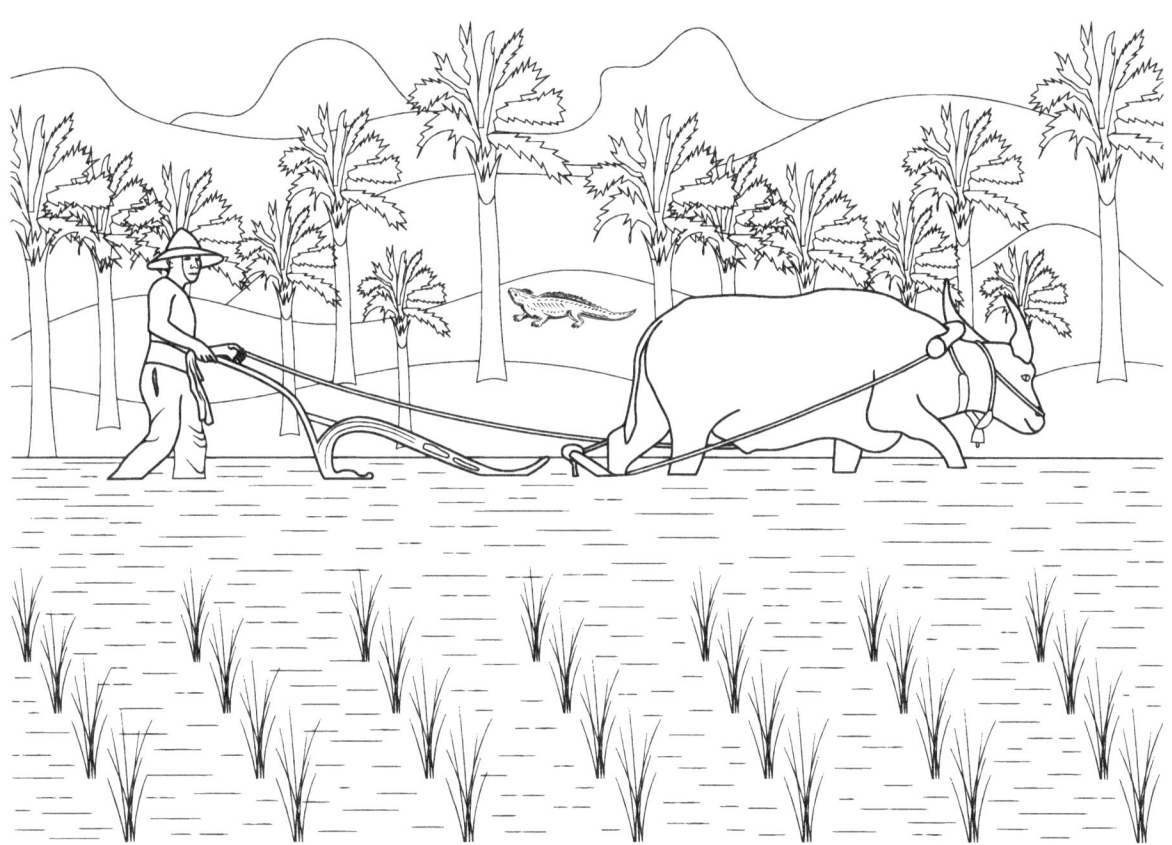

Find 4 differences in the picture below.

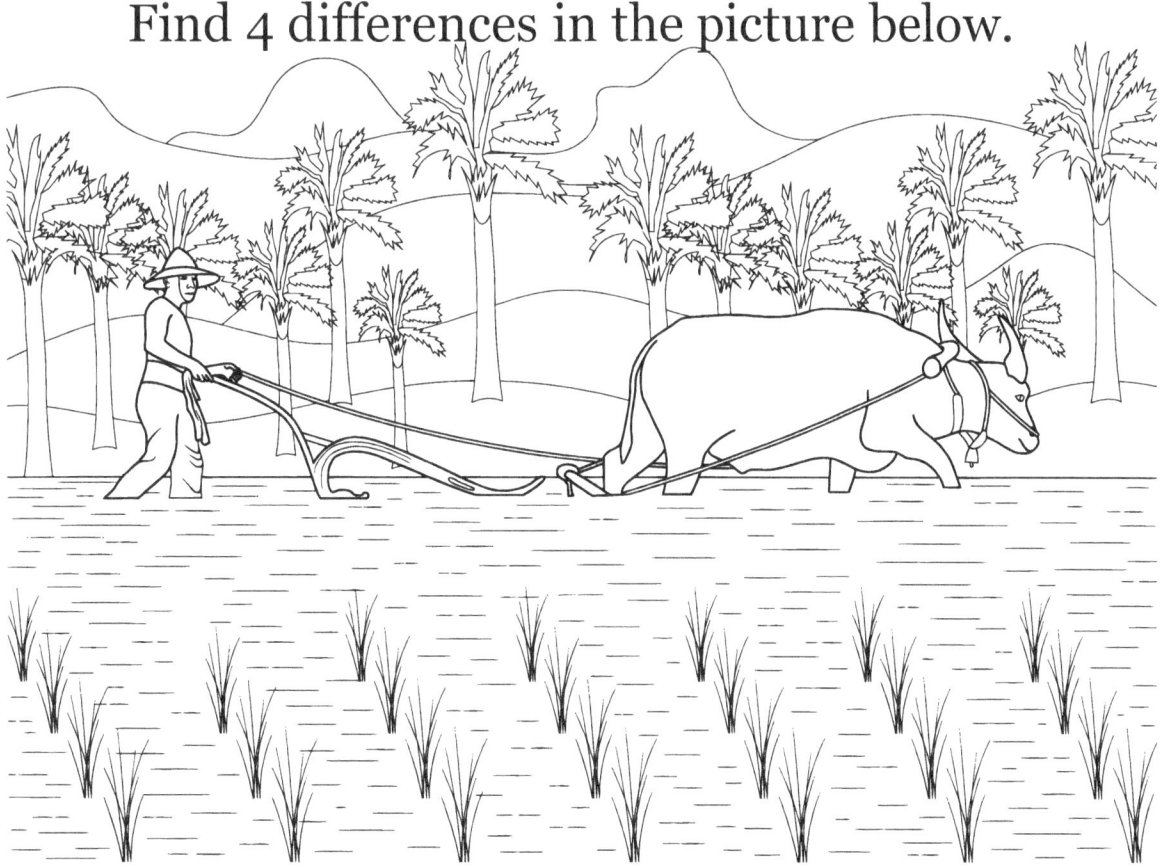

Puzzle 24

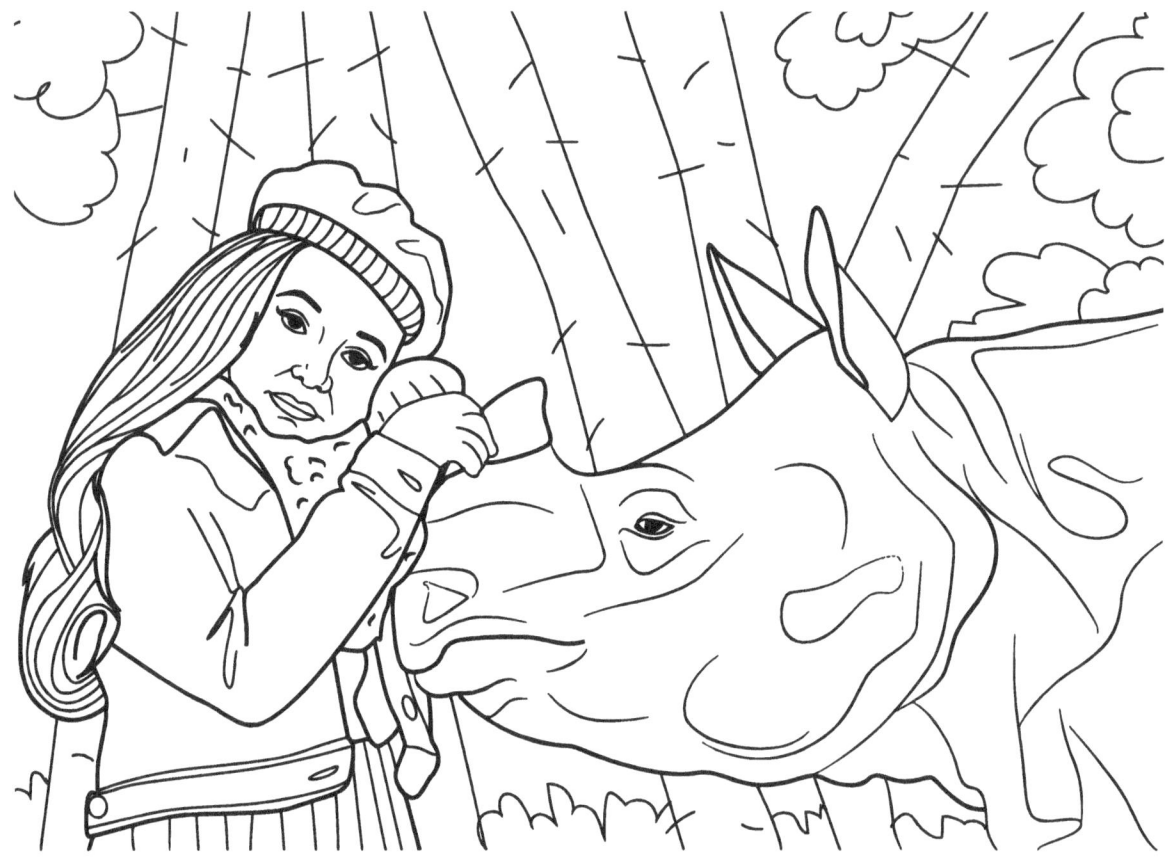

Find 5 differences in the picture below.

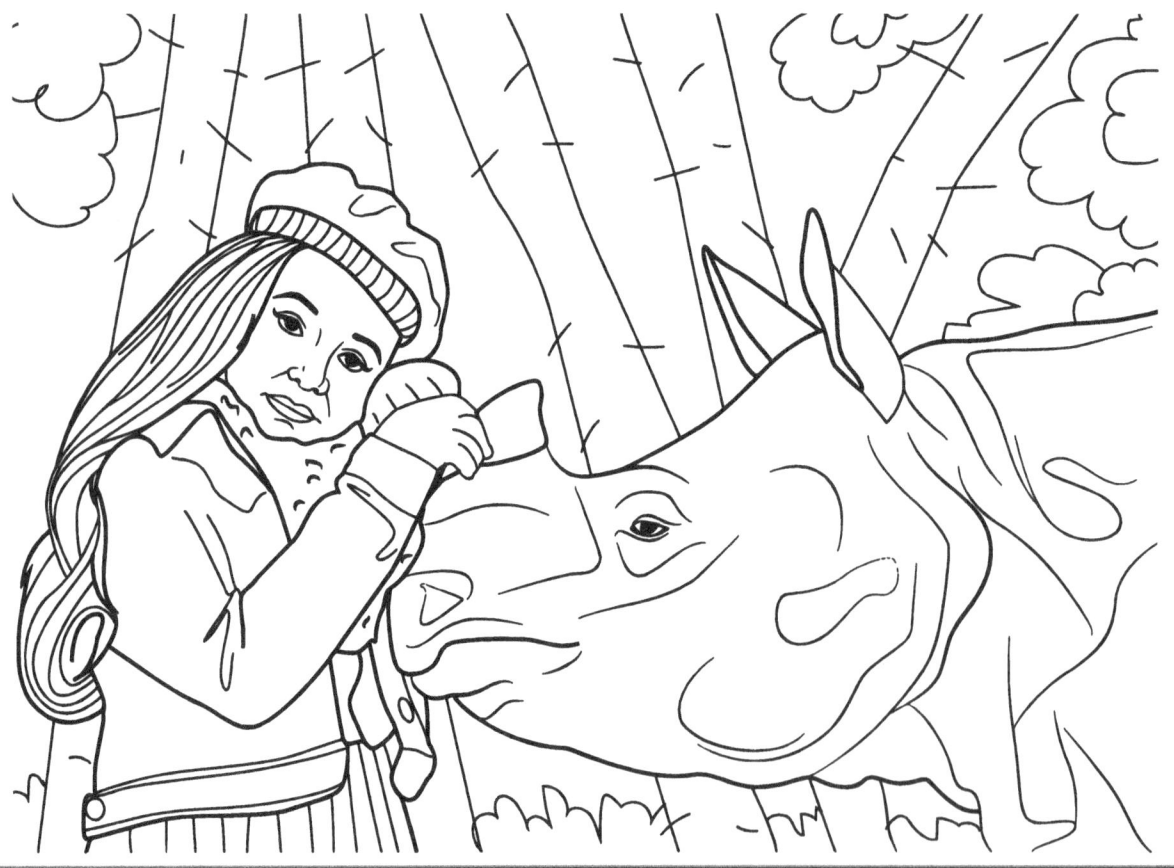

Puzzle 25

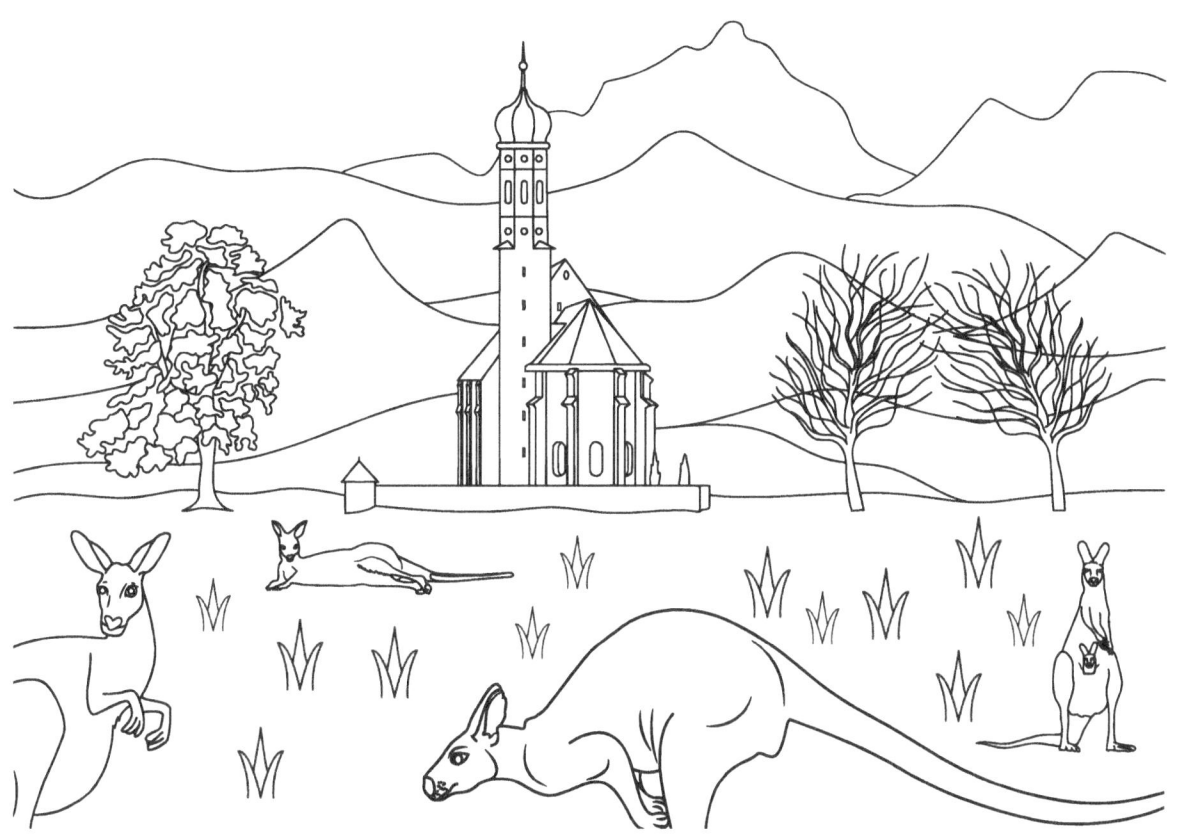

Find 1 difference in the picture below.

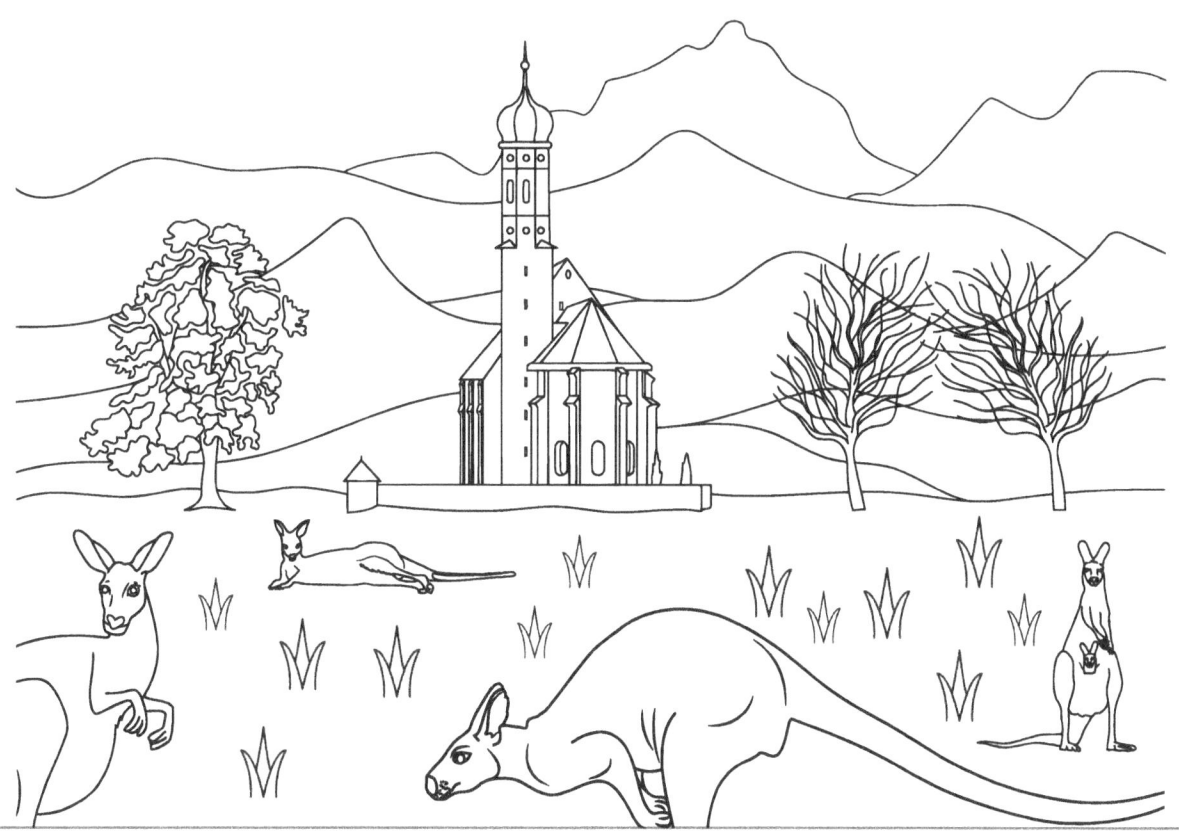

Picture Puzzles Spot the Difference

Solutions

Puzzle 1

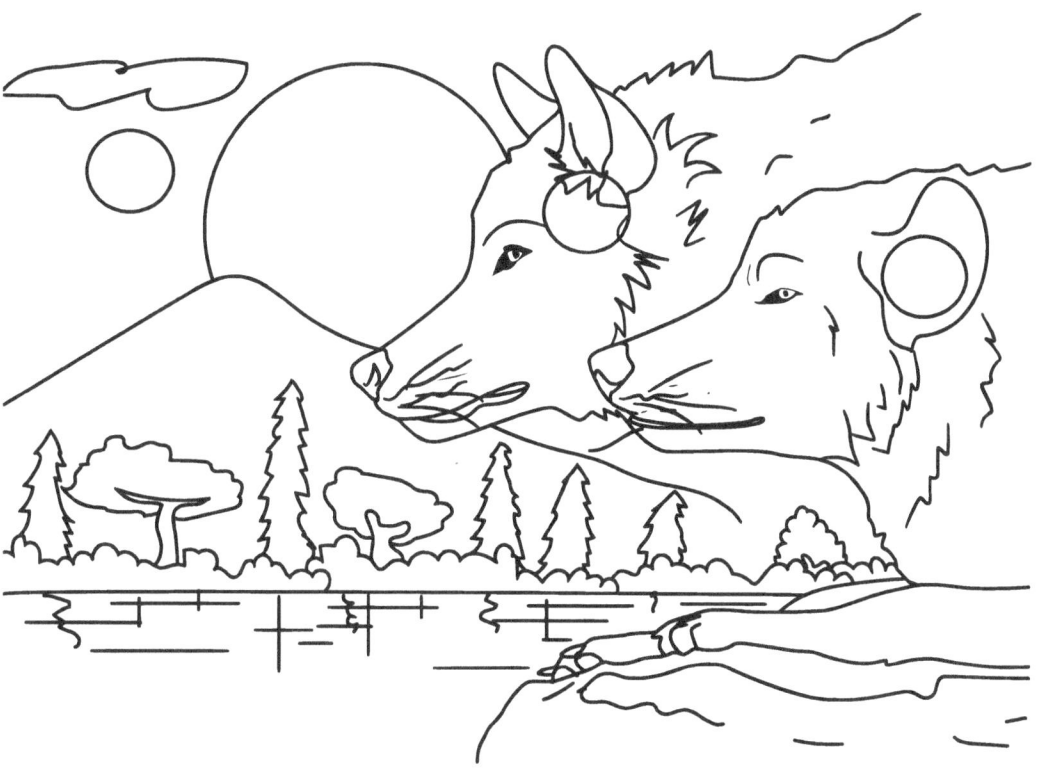

Puzzle 2

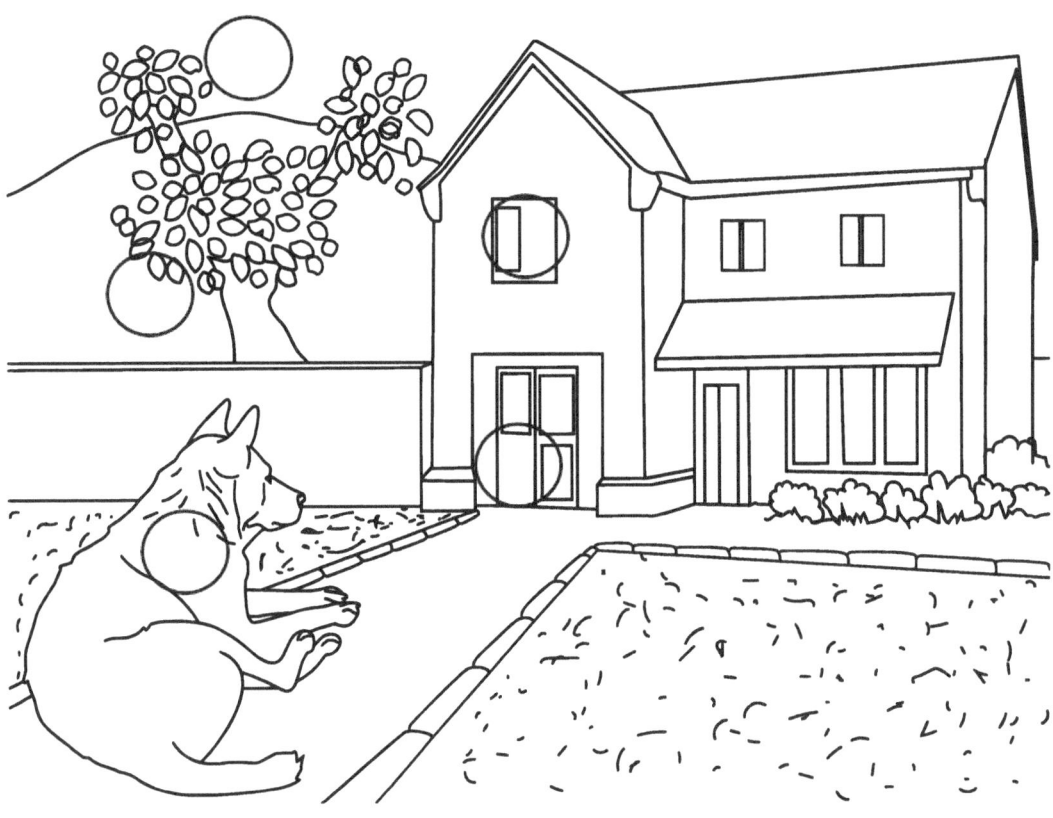

Puzzle 3

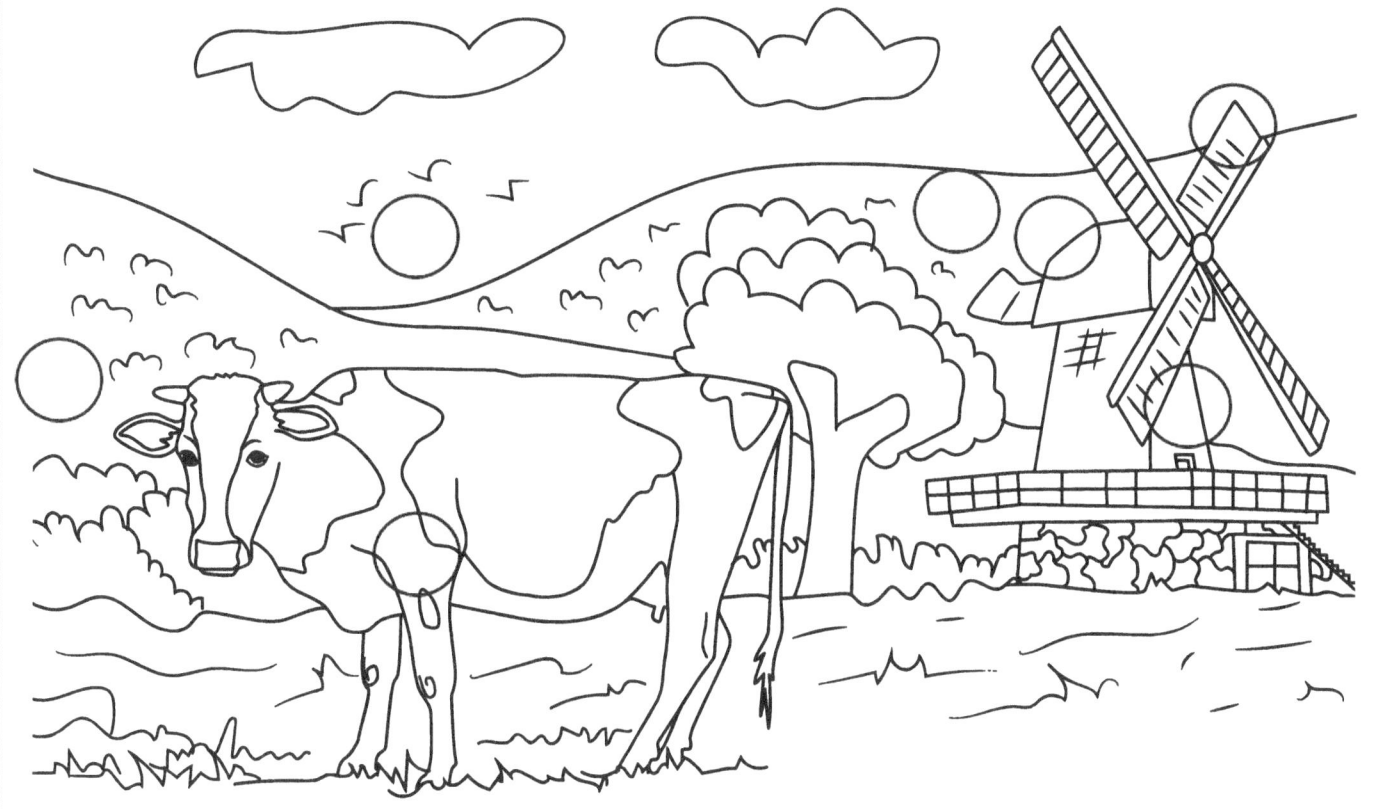

Puzzle 4

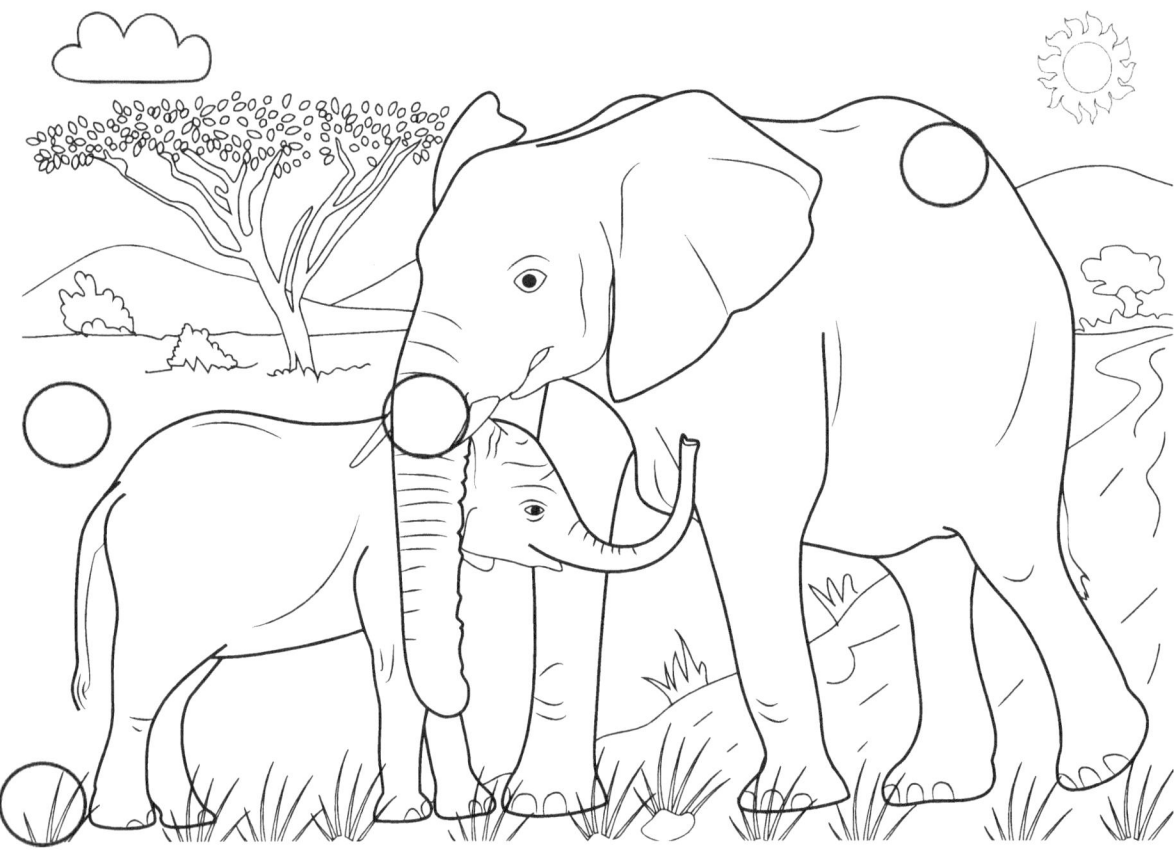

Puzzle 5

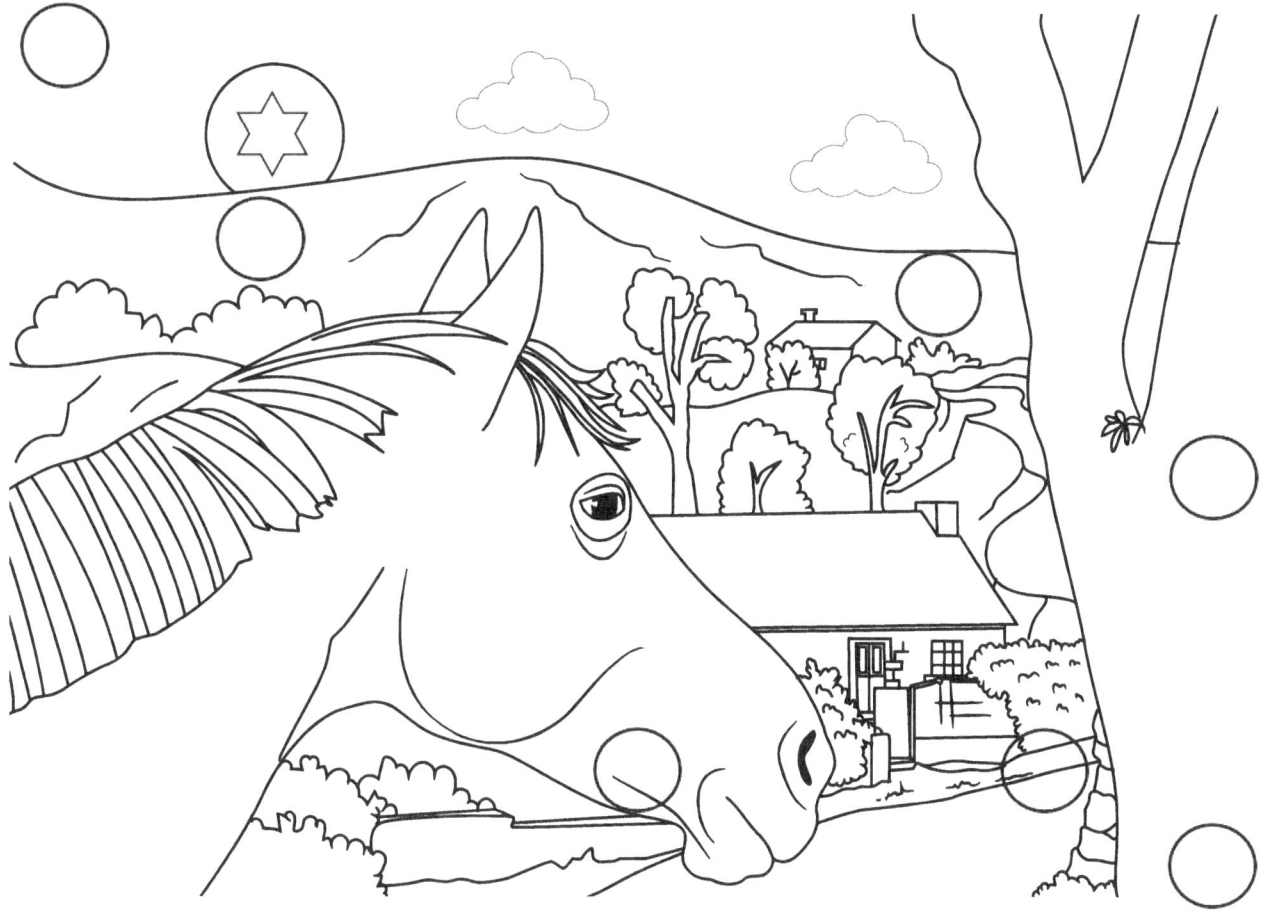

Puzzle 6

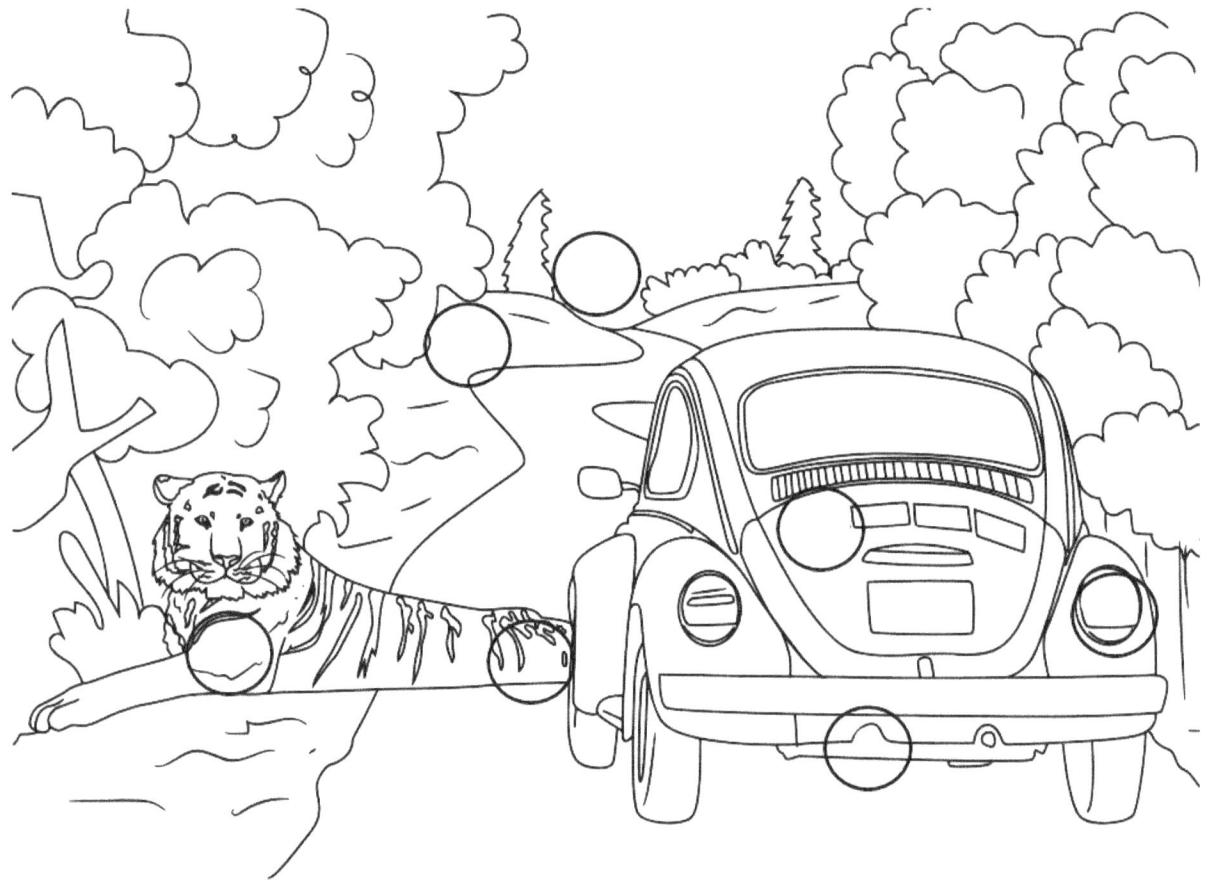

Puzzle 7

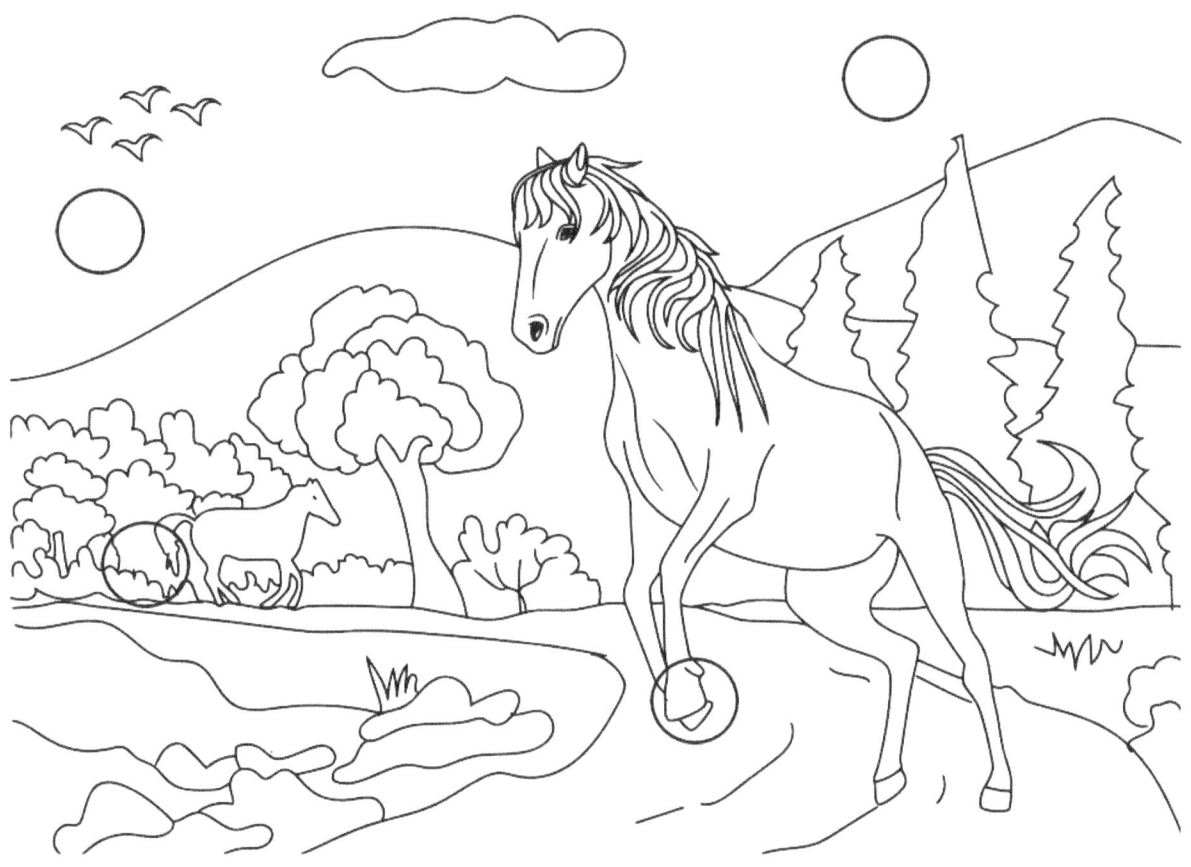

Puzzle 8

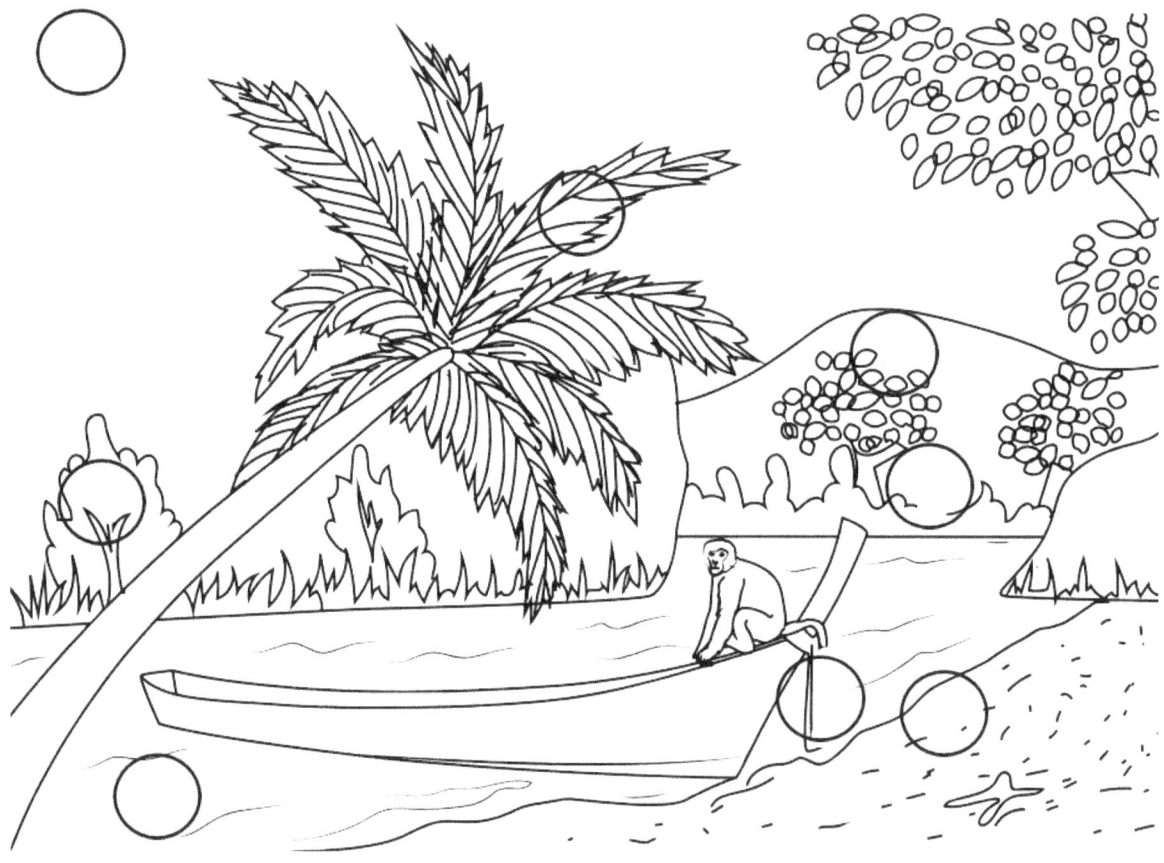

Puzzle 9

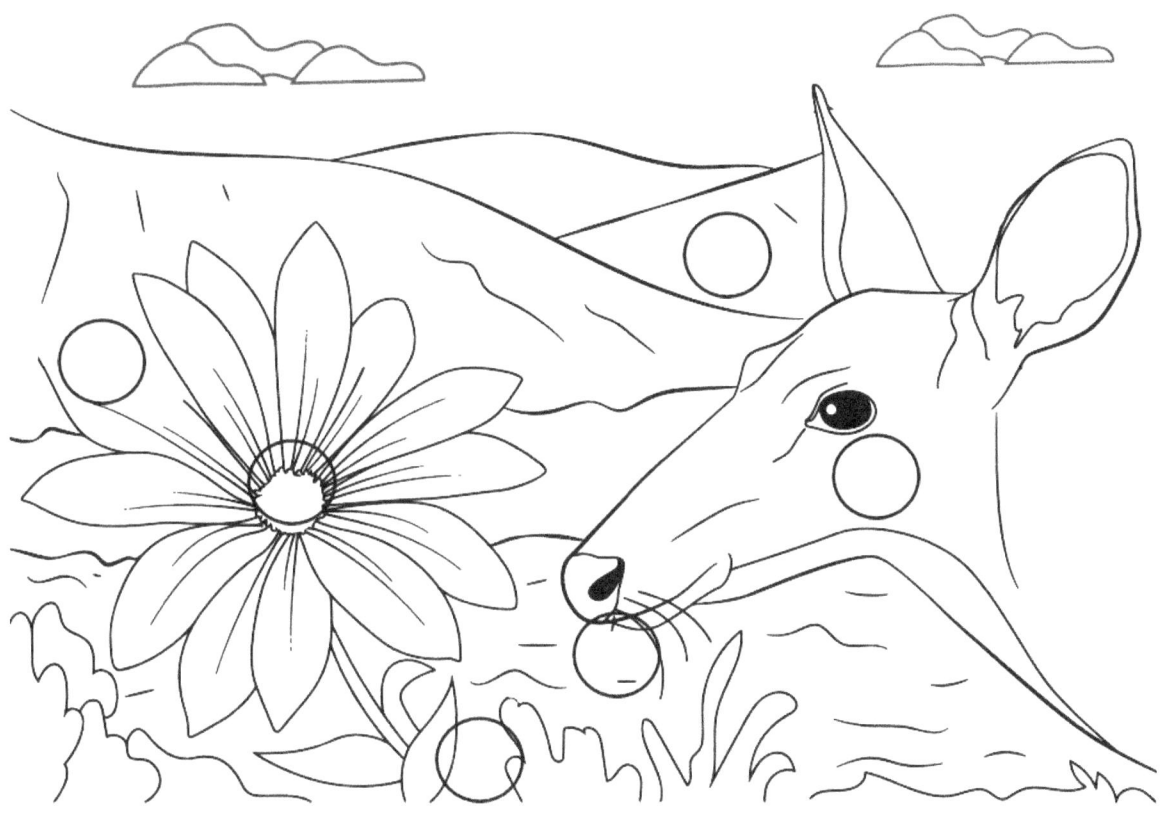

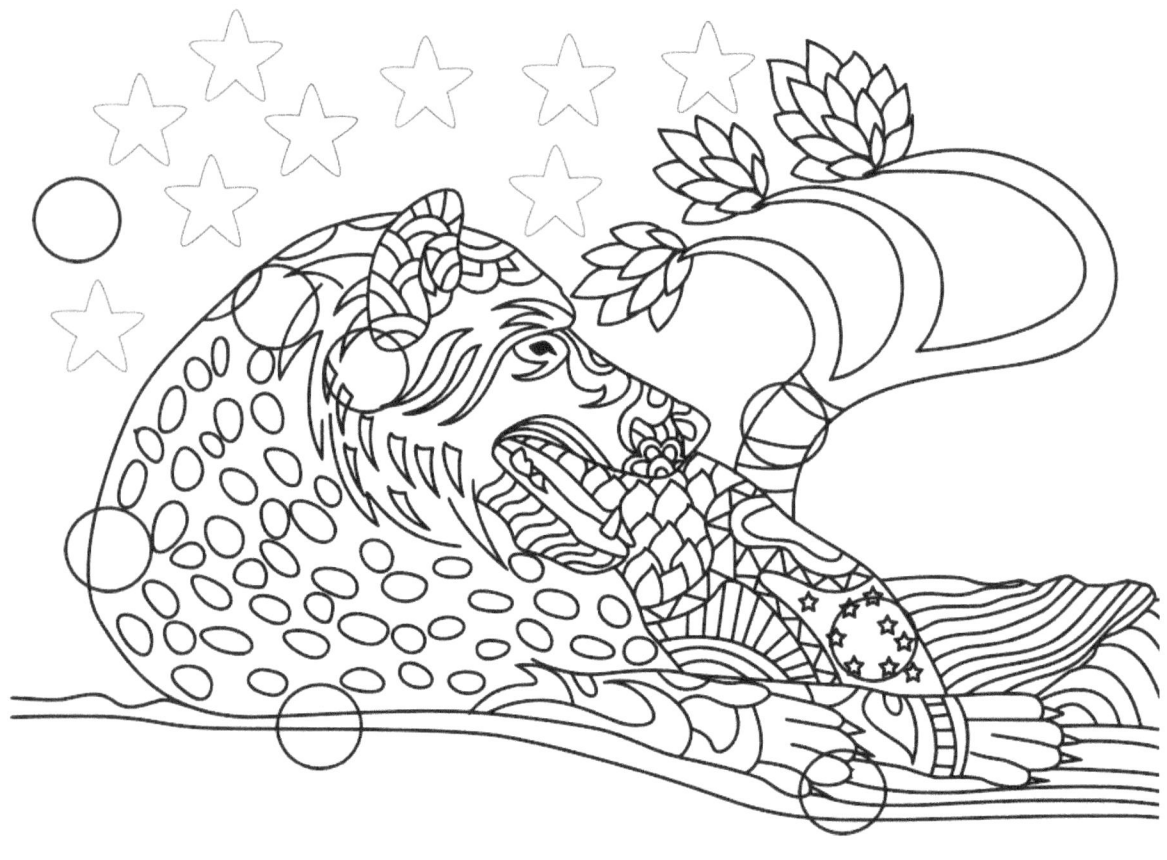

Puzzle 11

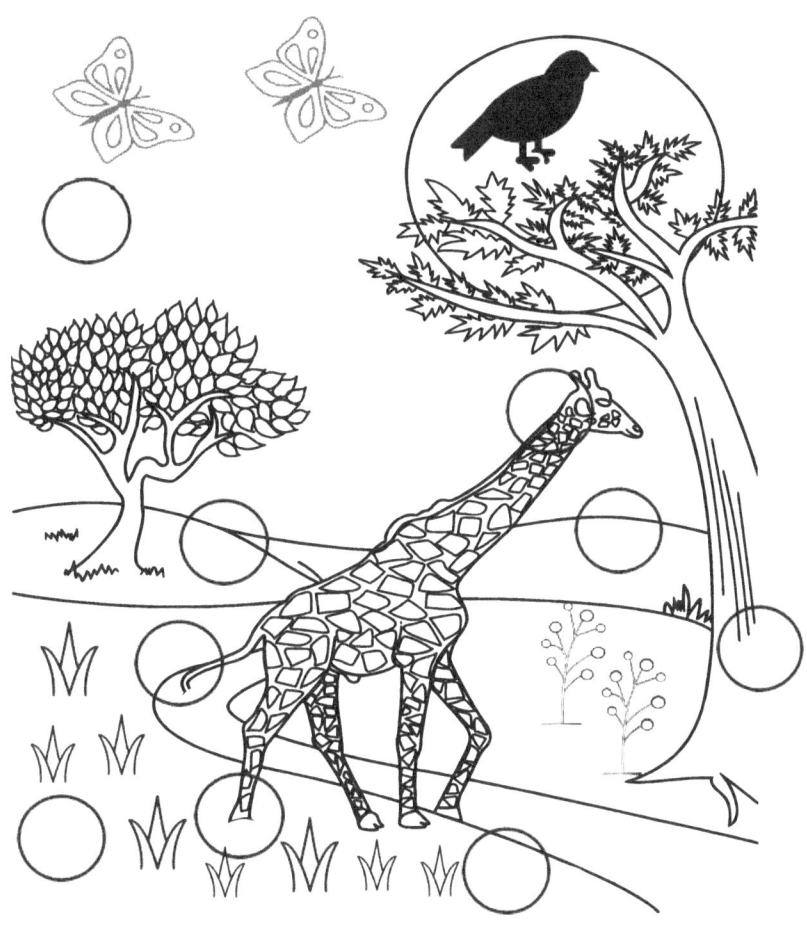

Puzzle 12

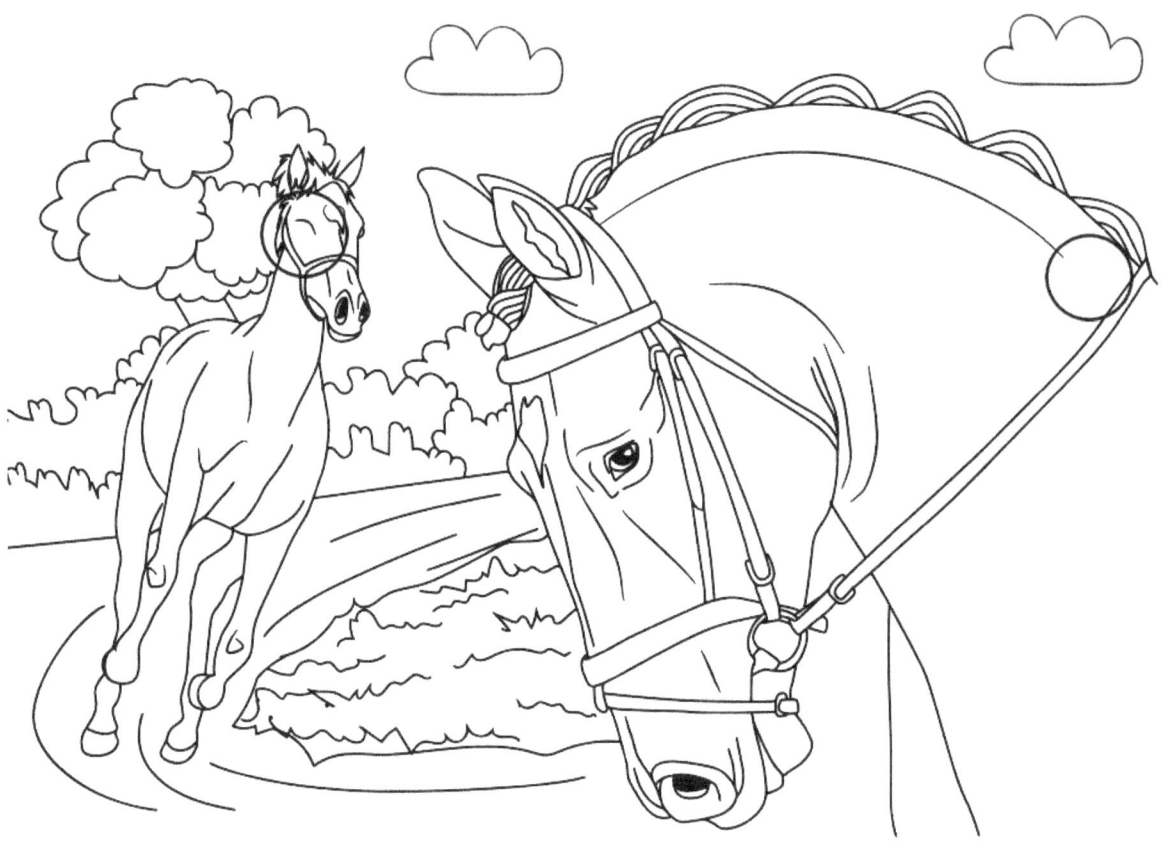

Puzzle 13

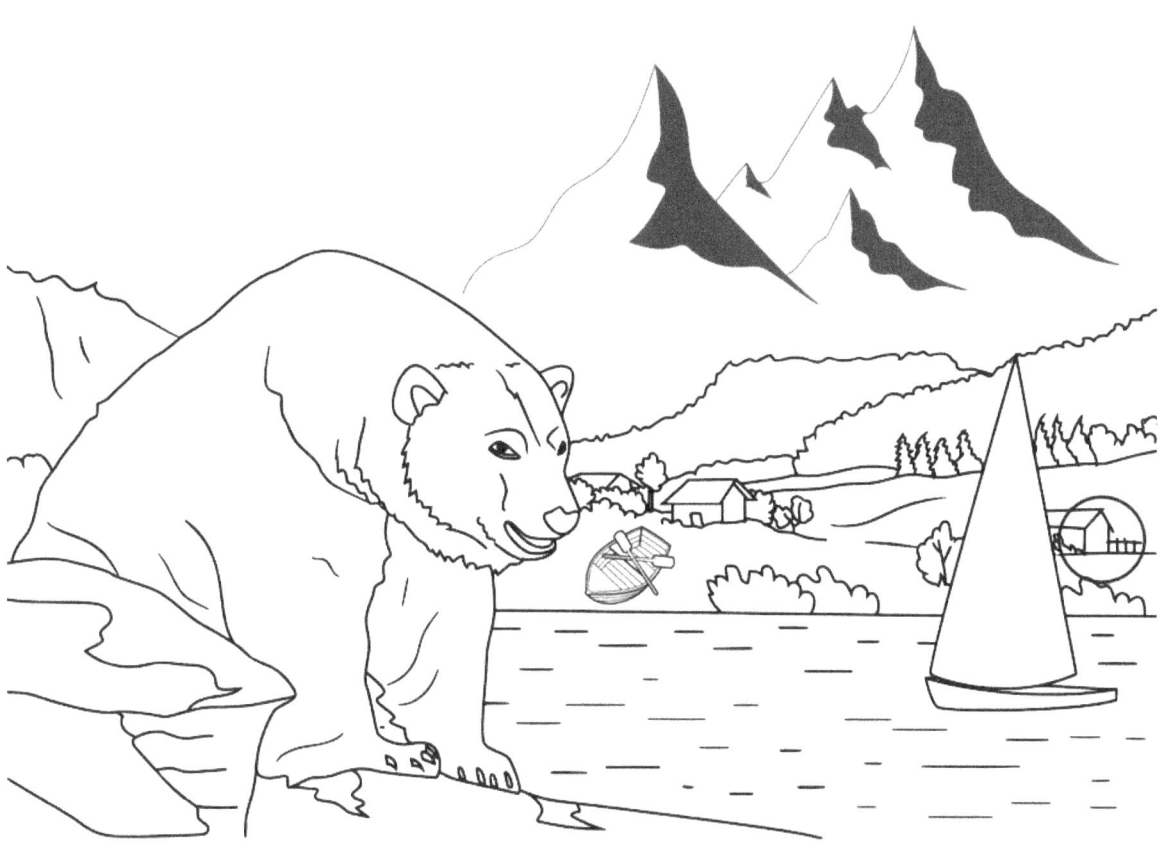

Puzzle 14

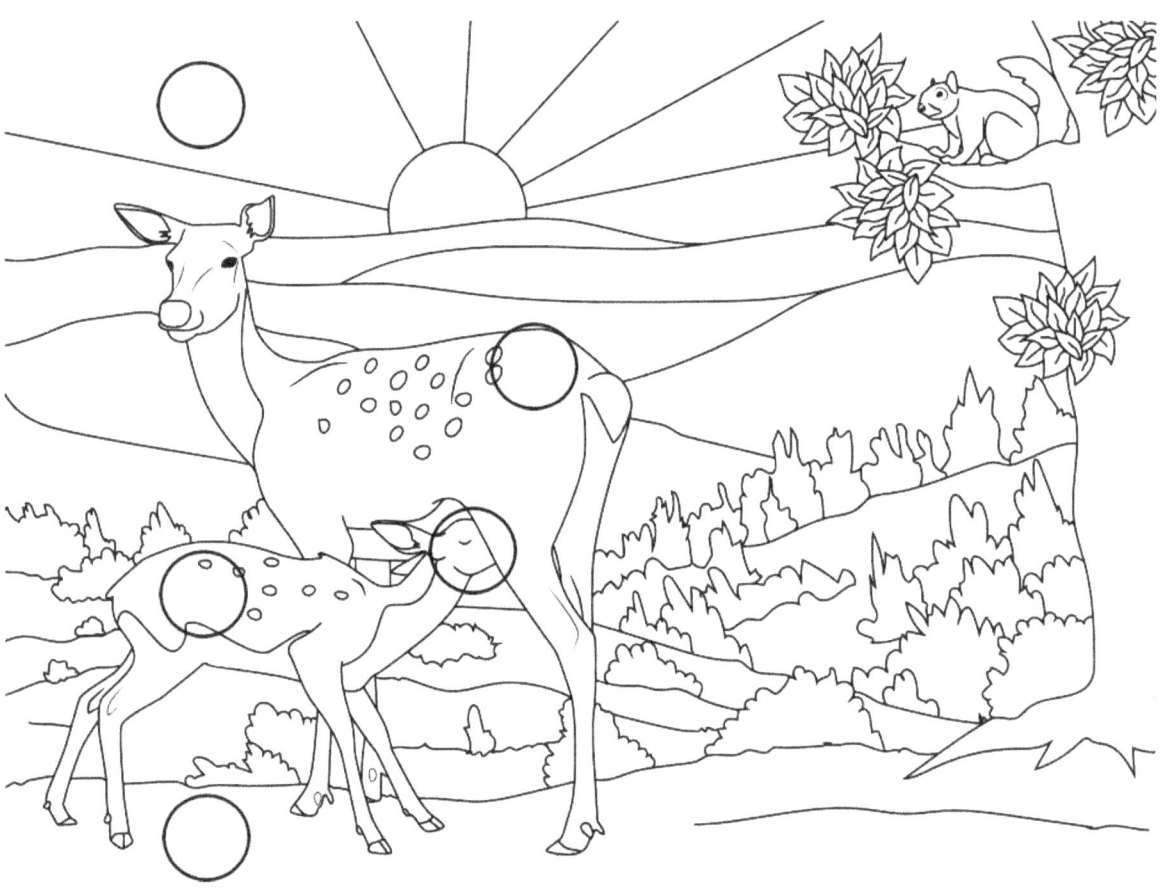

Puzzle 15

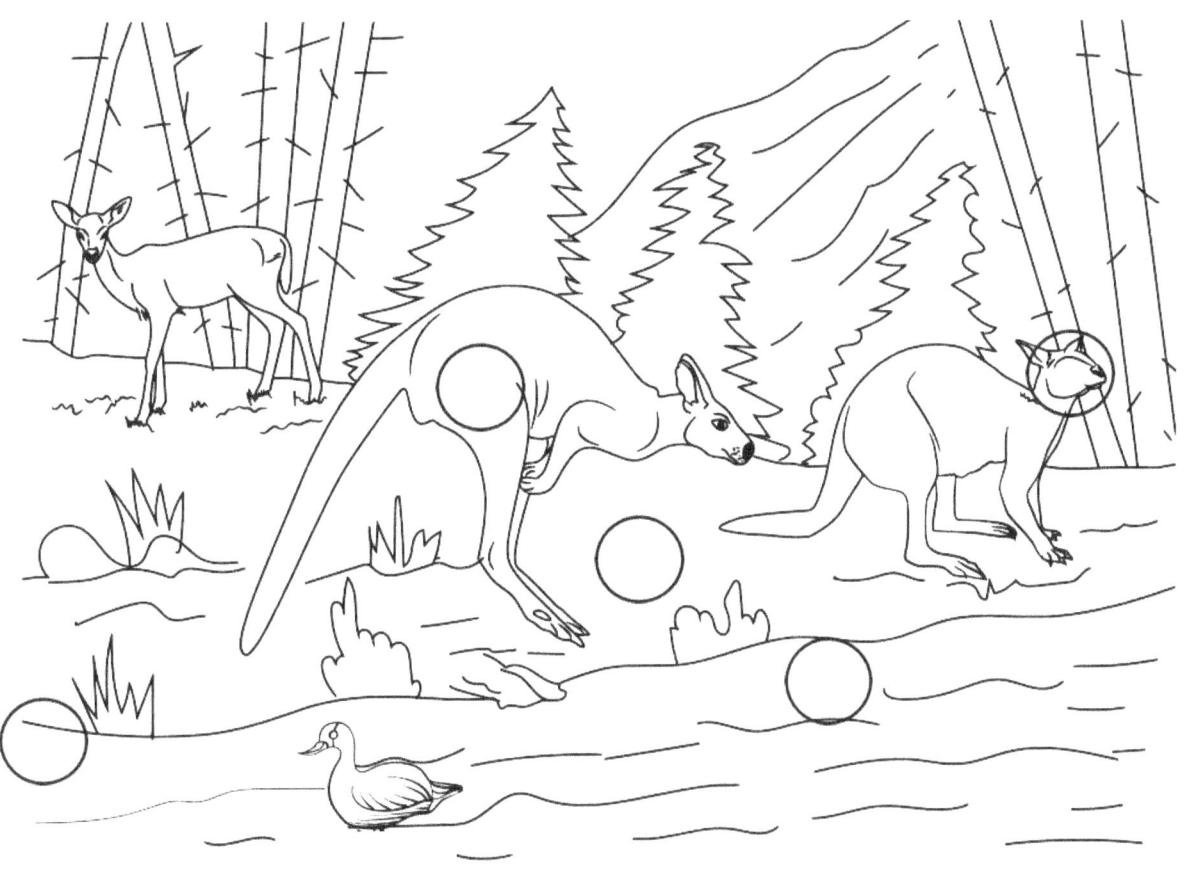

Puzzle 16

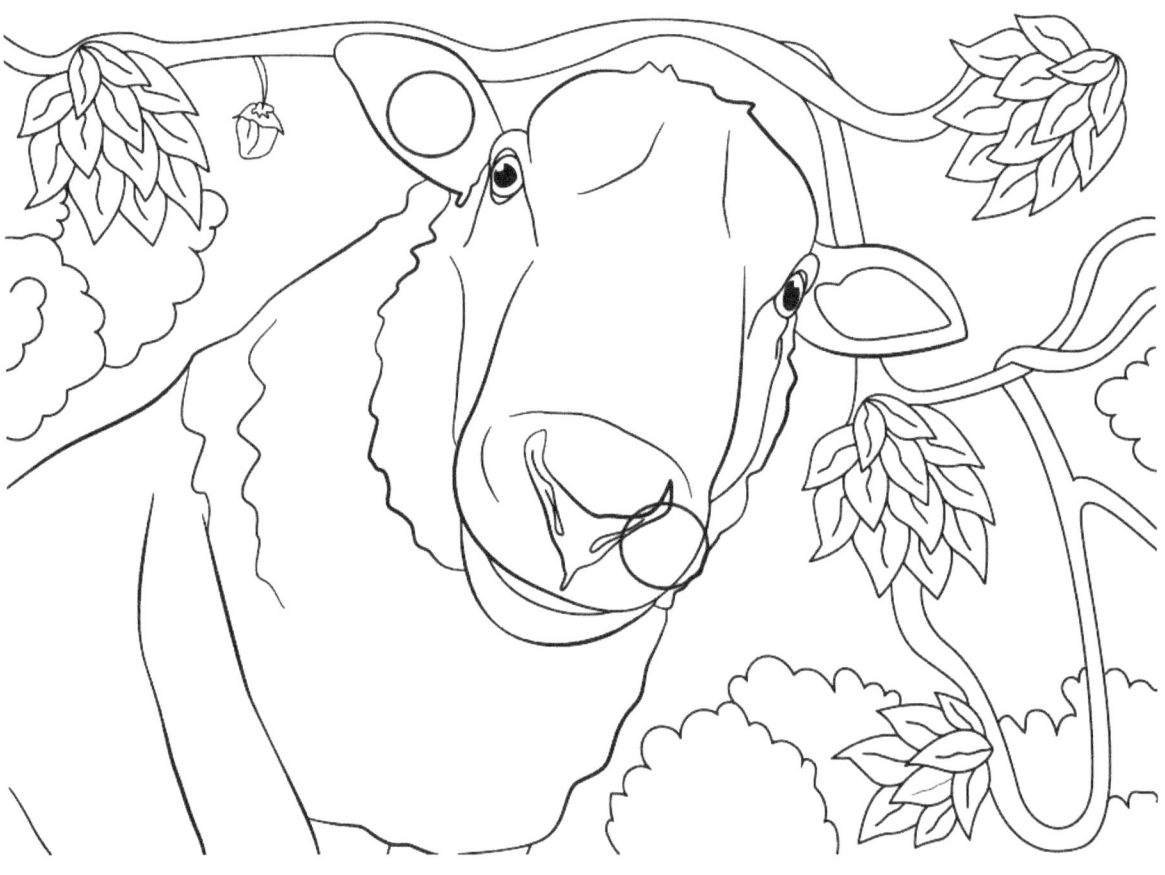

Puzzle 17

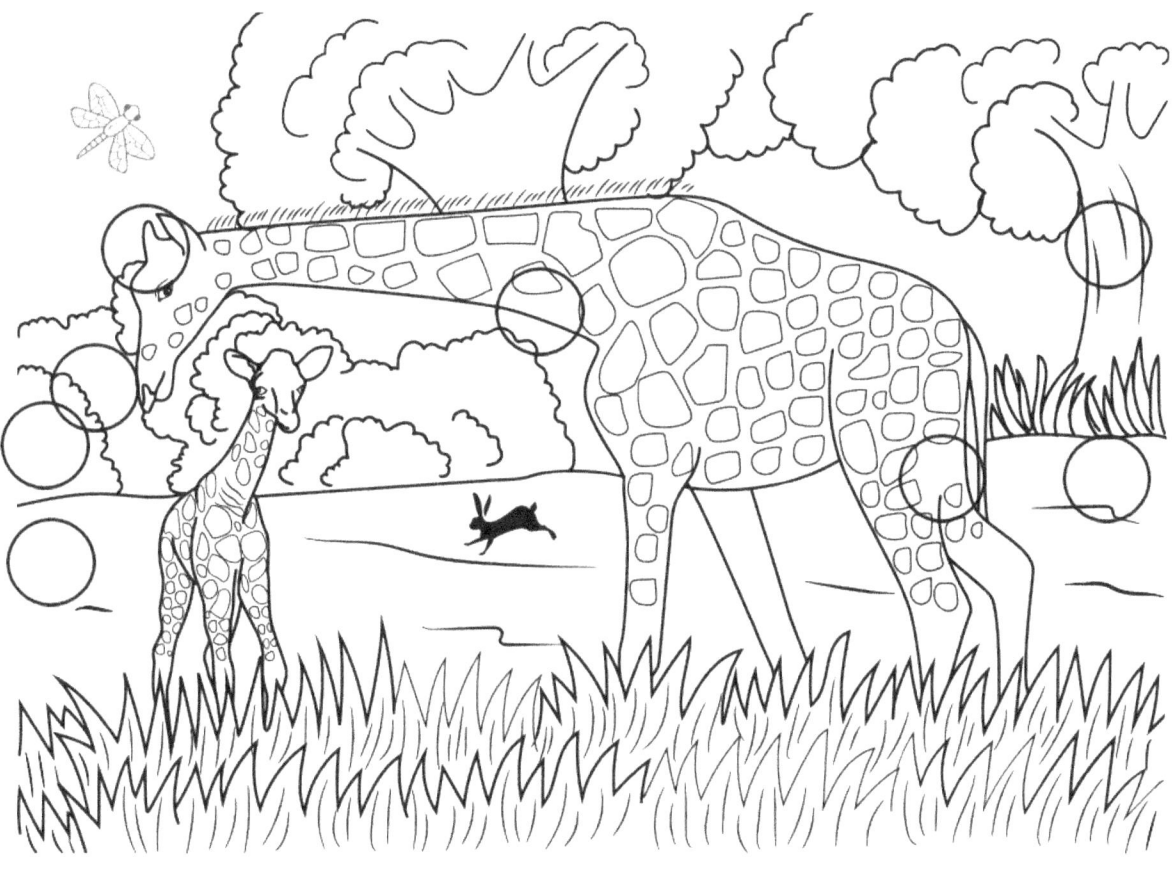

Puzzle 18

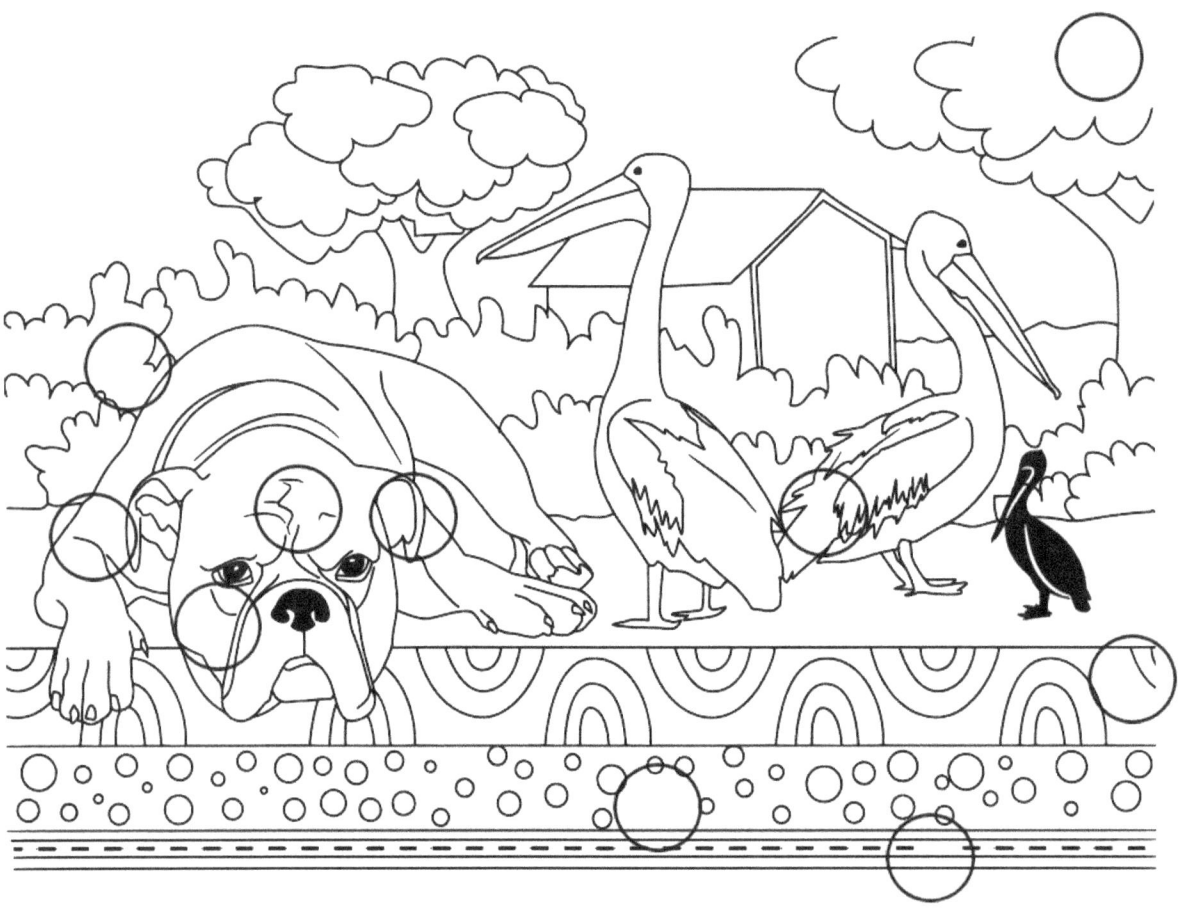

Puzzle 19

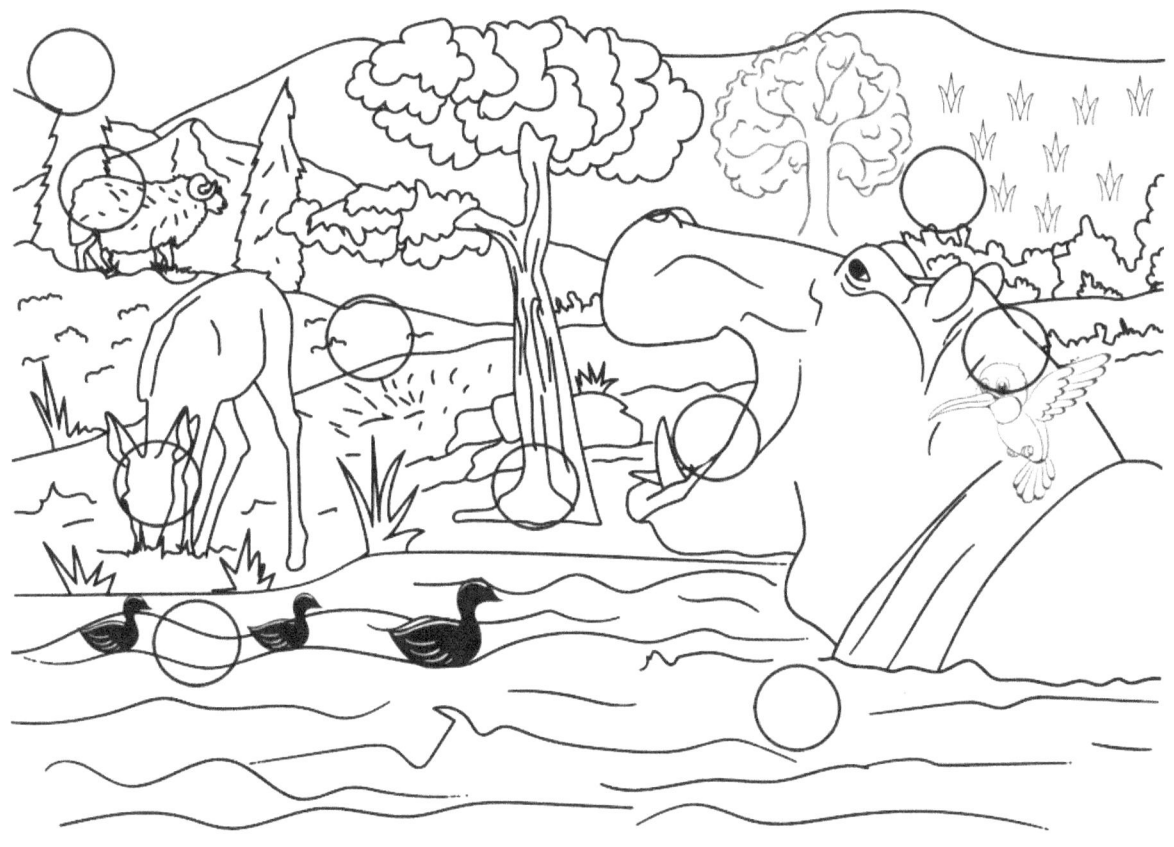

Puzzle 20

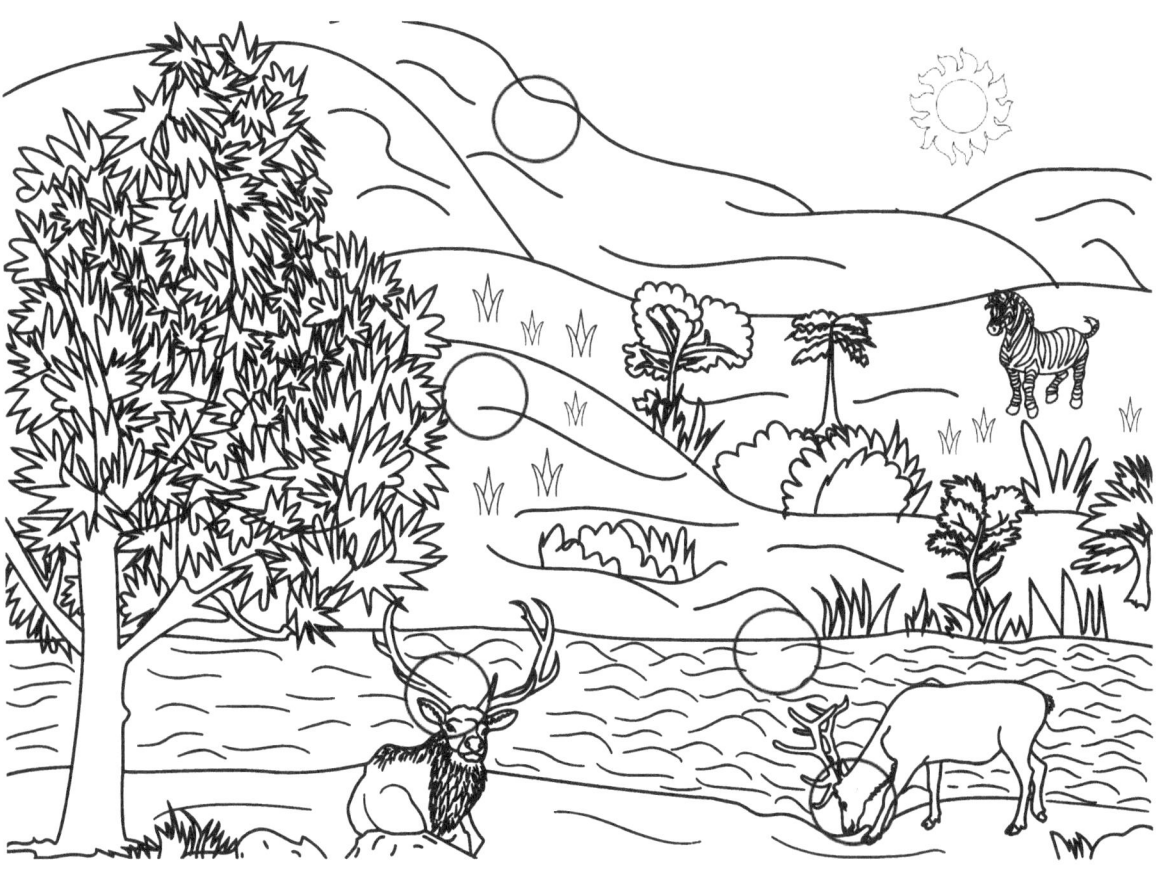

Puzzle 21

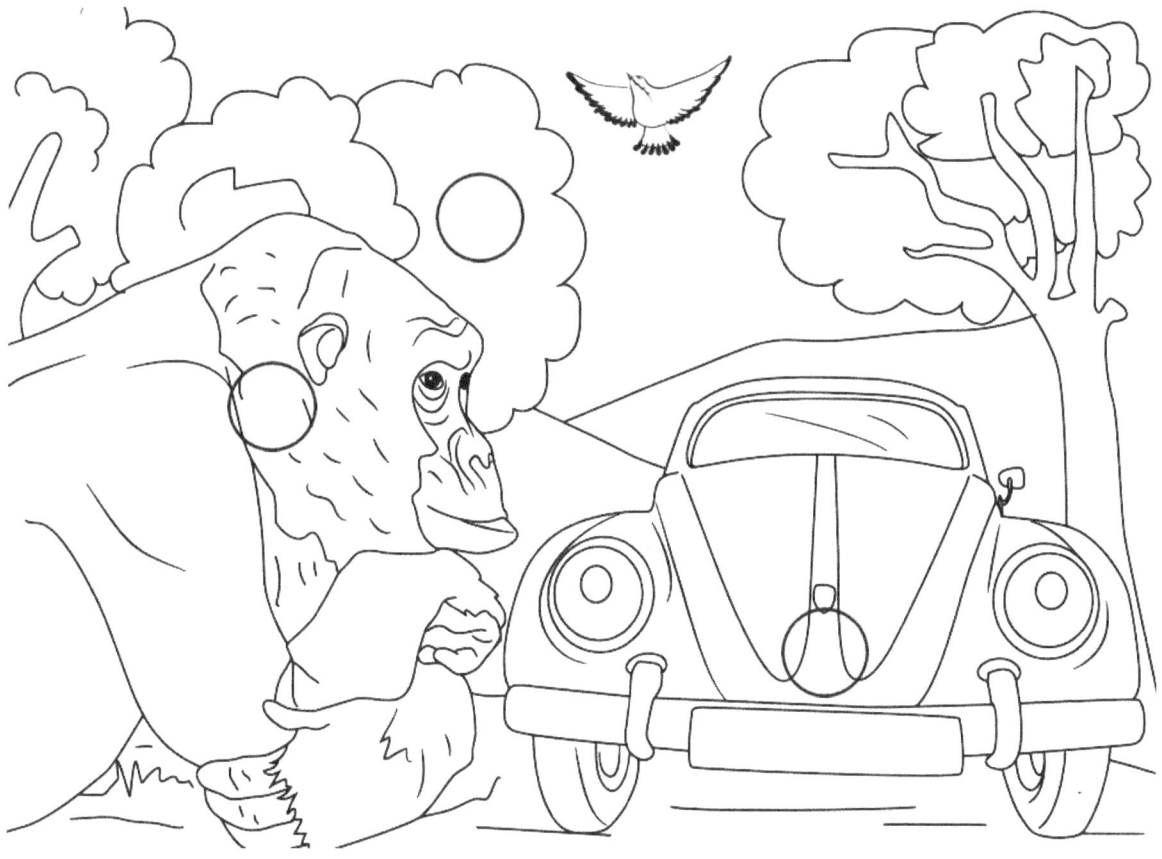

Puzzle 22

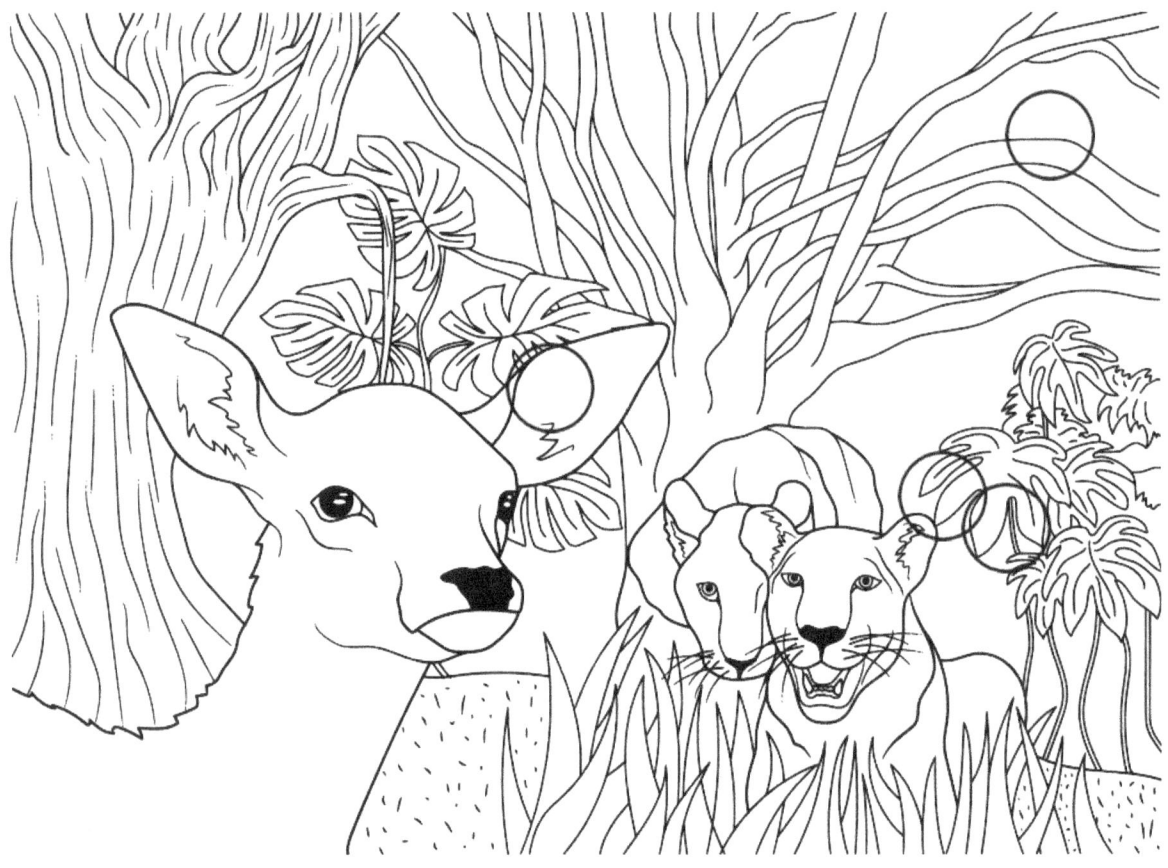

Puzzle 23

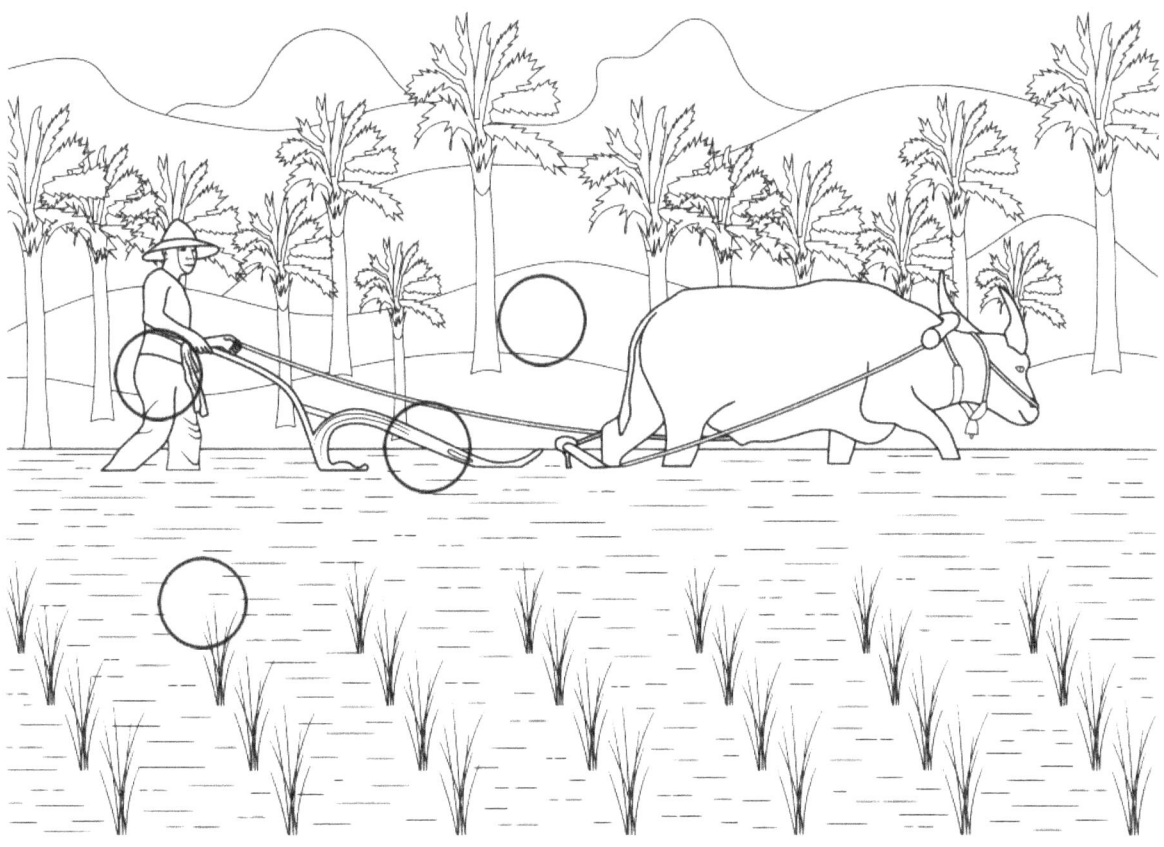

Puzzle 24

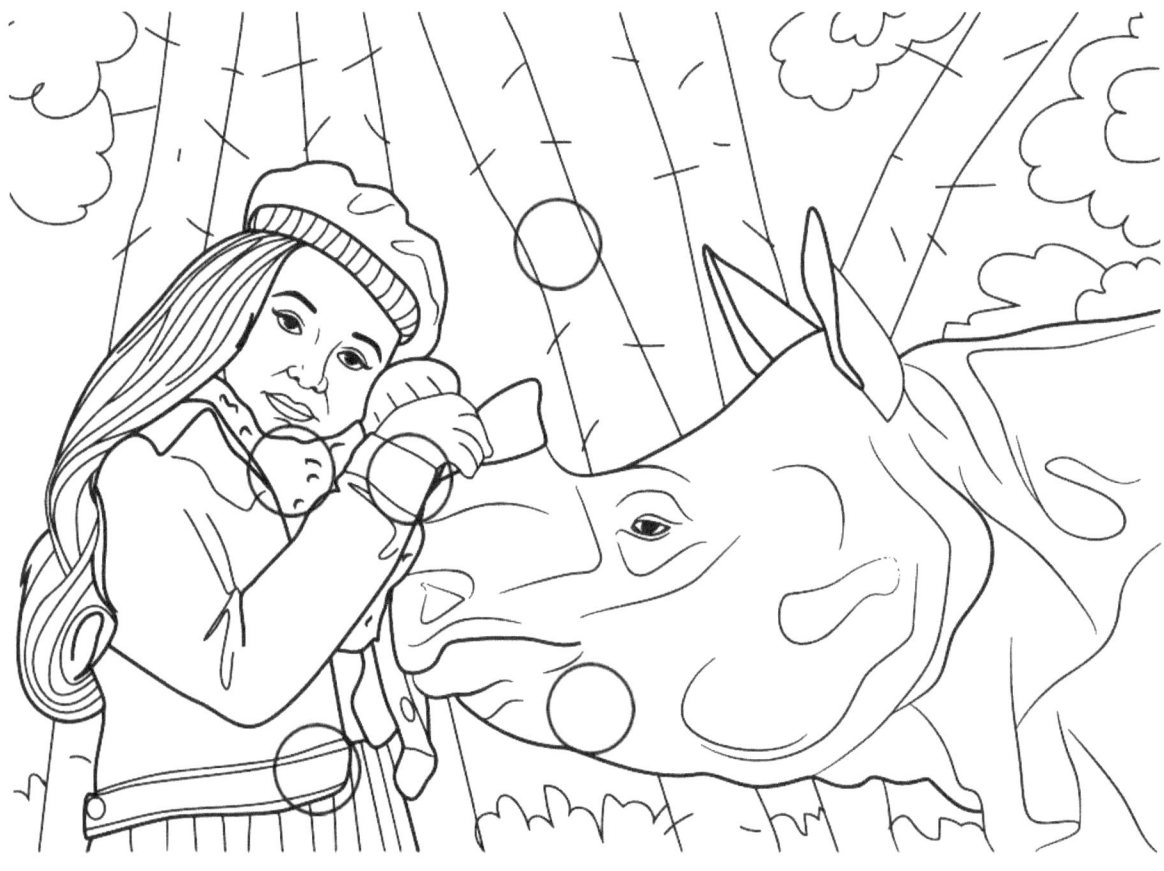

Puzzle 25

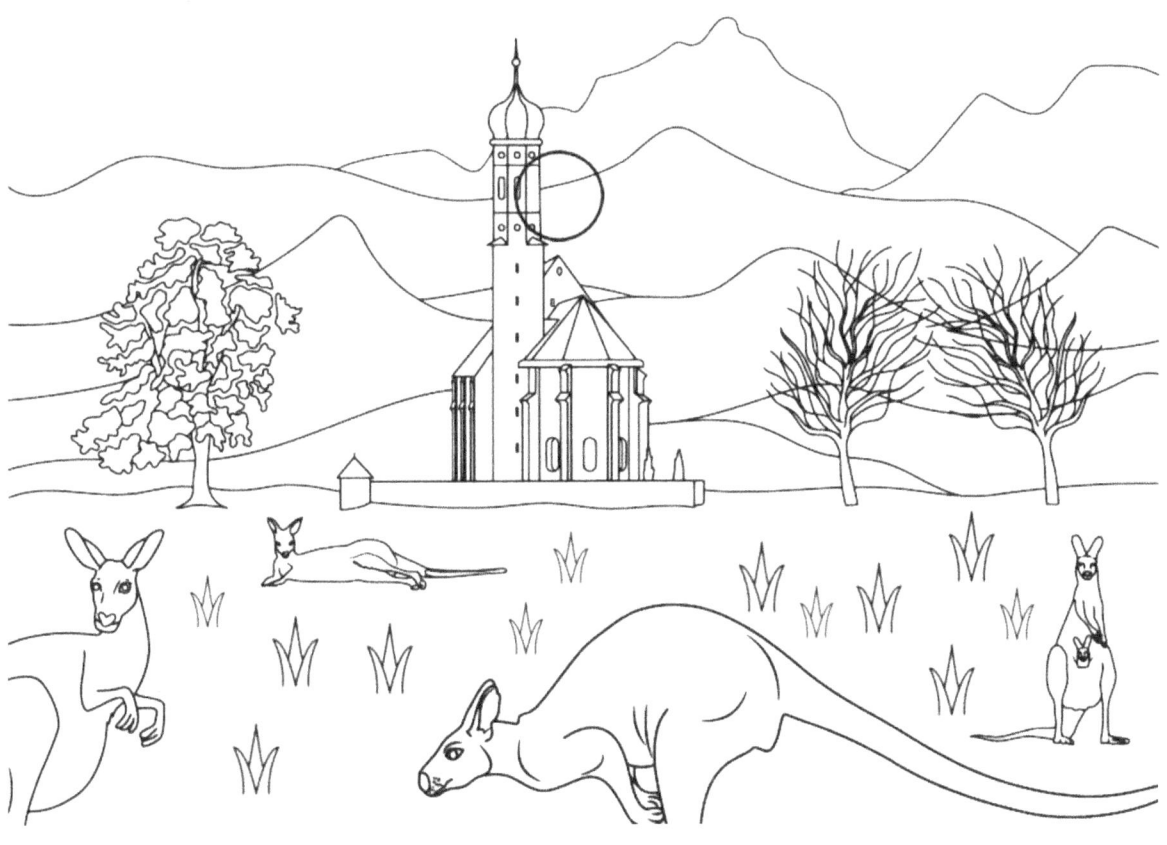